# HIDDEN ASSETS

## Connecting the Past to the Future of St. Louis

### Edited by

**Richard Rosenfeld**

© 2006 by the Missouri Historical Society Press
All rights reserved 10 09 08 07 06 1 2 3 4 5

Library of Congress Cataloging-in-Publication Data

Hidden assets : connecting the past to the future of St. Louis / edited by Richard
Rosenfeld.
        p. cm.
    Summary: "After reviewing the area's performance on the standard indicators of
growth and development, this volume identifies several hidden assets that distinguish St.
Louis from other metropolitan areas"--Provided by publisher.
    Includes bibliographical references and index.
    ISBN-13: 978-1-883982-56-0 (pbk. : alk. paper)
    ISBN-10: 1-883982-56-1 (pbk. : alk. paper)
    1. Saint Louis (Mo.)--Economic conditions. 2. Industries--Missouri--Saint Louis. I.
Rosenfeld, Richard. II. Missouri Historical Society.
    HC108.S2H53 2006
    330.9778'66--dc22
                                        2006000215


Distributed by University of Missouri Press

Designed by Creativille, Inc.
Printed and bound by Sheridan Books

# Table of Contents

# Foreword

I have lived in St. Louis longer than I have lived anywhere else, except for my hometown on the Upper Peninsula of Michigan. That town is imprinted deeply and irrevocably in me, and it is the place that nurtured me into adulthood. But St. Louis is now my home, my place of choice, and I believe I know it as well as anyone, certainly better than I have known any other place. My very being is entangled with this place, its beauties and its burdens, its foibles and its strengths.

While admitting our region's problems and actively seeking community solutions, I take delight in St. Louis's idiosyncrasies. The aroma of St. Louis is down by the brewery as the odor of the hops rides the breeze; it's in several parts of the city when the summer barbeques are fired up. I taste St. Louis in a Ted Drewes sundae, and where else can you find real gooey butter cake or the original toasted ravioli? I revel in the riot of chrysanthemums in the fall, the budding trees in spring, even the nearly visible waves of wet heat in the summer and the reputation we justly have for change-a-minute weather in any season. I feel a rush of gratitude when I look from my window in the History Museum out over Forest Park, the gem of our city's magnificent park system. What other urban area can claim anything like this civic-minded beauty, this history-laden public oasis, this special spot that so truly belongs to our whole community?

The St. Louis region can boast of its universities, libraries, museums, zoo, symphony, theaters from the Fabulous Fox and the Black Rep to the small professional companies and their talented community counterparts, a full list of eating establishments for every appetite and budget. We have the river, the mighty Mississippi, that strong brown god T. S. Eliot invoked, and we are at last paying attention to it. We have sports and music and poetry. These, and many more, are the beloved traits and features that we can include among our "hidden assets."

We have history, a tale too often told by the "winners" and delivered to the general populace but now seriously becoming a story to which all of us are contributing. This narrative of our past can, when properly employed, help us and those who come after us to a better future.

We have, I certainly believe, the spirit of St. Louis, and I am pleased that the Missouri Historical Society and MHS Press are part of this undertaking that reveals some of those hidden assets. This is indeed a spirit St. Louis and its regional community can understand and proclaim.

ROBERT R. ARCHIBALD, PH.D.
PRESIDENT, MISSOURI HISTORICAL SOCIETY

# Preface

"Action and reaction, ebb and flow, trial and error, change—this is the rhythm of living. Out of our over-confidence, fear; out of our fear, clearer vision, fresh hope. And out of hope, progress." These are the words of Bruce Barton, a former U.S. congressman from New York. He might have been talking about our own metropolitan region—St. Louis is a city, like all major cities, that has seen great change over its history.

When the Public Policy Research Center (PPRC) envisioned a book series, it was change that we were after. We wanted something that would illuminate the St. Louis metropolitan area's evolutions and revolutions over time. *Metromorphosis* seemed the perfect name for the book series. We wanted a series that would approach the region from many angles—from the history of its industry, its dynamic entertainment scene, the waxing and waning of its enthusiasm for sports, its finesse with ever-changing technology, its watersheds and parks, its transportation transformation, the shifting of its urban borders and the expansion of its suburbs, right down to the very fabric of its streets and buildings. Through this mélange, the human story of the region emerges, and ultimately the region's change is about people. As Henry David Thoreau said, "Things do not change; we change." The St. Louis Metromorphosis Book Series aims to capture this legacy of transformation with a thorough documentation and analysis of economic, social, political, and historical aspects of the St. Louis metropolitan area.

The term *metromorphosis* has a history with PPRC. I originally used it as the title of a 2001 photography exhibition. The exhibit paired black and white photographs documenting changes in the St. Louis built environment. Through these images I explored the exterior architecture of office buildings and theaters, residences, churches, and transportation infrastructure. Each pair offered a visual comparison—one building that was older and architecturally distinct, juxtaposed with a contemporary building that was, more often than not, architecturally unremarkable. The change in the metropolitan built environment over time was striking.

The first book in the St. Louis Metromorphosis Book Series bore the same name and, like the photo exhibit, also offered a striking view of the differences between "then" and "now." Published in 2004 in collaboration with the Missouri Historical Society, St. *Louis Metromorphosis: Past Trends and Future Directions* provided a sophisticated, quantitative analysis of changes across the St. Louis region over the last five decades. Using data sets extending back as long as a century, twelve scholars from four area universities analyzed key policy issues and trends.

After the publication of this book, the PPRC Advisory Committee, under the direction of Dr. Robert Archibald, approved the concept of a series by the same name. This book is the second in the series. *Hidden Assets: Connecting the Past to the Future of St. Louis* looks beyond the surface to explore several unexpected treasures that distinguish St. Louis from seemingly comparable metropolitan areas. The book focuses on the potential for "non-obvious" development that might arise from the expansion and interaction of these assets, spurring regional vitality and growth. Another volume, about St. Louis plans, is in development, and several themes are being considered for a fourth volume.

This book series reaches out to a broad audience, with many different applications. We intend it to be a resource for scholars and academicians, those who will study our region and provide the analysis that comes before action. Residents will take a special interest in this series, both newcomers who are seeking to understand the dynamics of this region and longtime citizens who have witnessed some of the changes our series documents. The books hold national value as well, for they provide a resource for comparison to other cities with similar demographics and similar challenges. Each volume will be written in the distinct voice that comes with familiarity—people who know this city and this region.

Like all examinations of the past, however, this series does not offer a mere study of the region. Our hope for progress rests firmly on a clear vision of who we are and where we've been. Our true interest is understanding and shaping the future of our metropolitan area. This book series asks the questions, and offers some of the data, that will help planners, educators, residents, and politicians to consciously choose where we go from here.

MARK TRANEL

DIRECTOR, PUBLIC POLICY RESEARCH CENTER,

ASSISTANT RESEARCH PROFESSOR

OF PUBLIC POLICY ADMINISTRATION,

UNIVERSITY OF MISSOURI–ST. LOUIS

# Introduction

## Standard Measures and Hidden Assets

### Richard Rosenfeld

By many standard indicators, the St. Louis region is in a prolonged period of stagnation or decline. The urban core has suffered huge population loss. Fortune 500 companies have left the region. The central city has a large poverty population with all of the attendant social problems, including chronically high crime rates, high rates of family disruption, a failing public school system, and deteriorating public services. Several large inner-ring suburbs increasingly resemble the inner city, while the outer suburbs are characterized by unregulated sprawl. Residential patterns are highly segregated by race and wealth. Political fragmentation in the region and the corresponding absence of coherent and effective leadership are legendary. The list goes on. Based on these standard measures of strength, vitality, and growth, the region's future appears dim. But these are not the only indicators by which the present and possible future of the region, including the central city, should be assessed. The region contains many "hidden assets" that do not register on the standard metropolitan performance measures but, if effectively nurtured and promoted, augur a brighter future for St. Louis.

Several hidden assets distinguish St. Louis from other metro areas, including areas that rank higher on the standard measures. A partial list of such assets would include, to name just ten: (1) an abundant, durable, and affordable housing stock; (2) many distinct and vibrant residential communities; (3) the resurgence of several commercial and entertainment areas (the Delmar Loop, South Grand area, Soulard, midtown, the West End, the "Club 'n Loft" area of downtown); (4) three major universities and several small universities; (5) a major medical complex; (6) a stellar and popular sports tradition; (7) beautiful and accessible parks; (8) dozens of distinctive architectural structures; (9) a major plant sciences facility and accompanying gardens; and (10) a historic and robust blues music tradition. Together, these assets create a distinctive mosaic of amenities and resources, the value of which merits assessment. The contributors to this volume highlight the historical and contemporary importance of several of these community assets and related aspects of the St. Louis region. They invite us to contemplate the tradition and sheer beauty of St. Louis architecture; the lure of the rivers; the promise of new research partnerships; the centrality of the automobile and a strong manufacturing base to the area's development; the bravura sports traditions, both professional and amateur; the persistence and vitality of live blues music; and the unheralded significance of neighborhood institutions for individual development and community stability. The volume reminds us that St. Louis's best chance for a bright future depends on forging creative connections with the past.

It will not be easy. Although this book's major premise is that the standard indicators of metropolitan vitality and growth do not determine the region's future, they cannot be ignored. Before considering some of St. Louis's hidden assets, it is worth examining the region's performance and progress on several of the standard economic and social measures by which cities and metropolitan areas are usually compared. The appendix presents several of these measures, drawn from the 1990 and 2000 U.S. censuses, for the fifty largest metropolitan areas in the nation with populations of one million or more.

# St. Louis on the Standard Performance Measures

St. Louis is the eighteenth largest U.S. metropolitan area, with a population of 2.6 million.[1] Based on the 2000 census, it ranks thirty-second among the fifty largest metropolitan areas in median household income; twenty-ninth in the percentage of the population age twenty-five

---

[1] The St. Louis metropolitan area consists of the city of St. Louis and the following fifteen Missouri and Illinois counties: Bond, Calhoun, Clinton, Franklin, Jefferson, Jersey, Lincoln, Macoupin, Madison, Monroe, St. Charles, St. Clair, St. Louis, Warren, and Washington.

and over with a bachelor, graduate, or professional degree; thirty-fourth in the rate of poverty; and twentieth in unemployment. St. Louis's violent crime rate places it twenty-third among the fifty largest metro areas in 2004 and thirtieth in property crime.[2] On these measures of economic and social well-being, St. Louis is in the middle of the distribution of the country's major metropolitan regions and occupies about the same position relative to other areas as it did in 1990. This is not a story of notable progress, but neither is it one of outright decay.

The St. Louis region is growing, but at a tepid pace. High-growth metro areas are characterized by burgeoning immigrant populations; immigrants go where the opportunities are. St. Louis ranks forty-eighth among the fifty largest metropolitan areas in the percentage of the population that is Hispanic and forty-fourth in the percentage that resided outside of the United States five years earlier. The St. Louis region actually fell several positions among the fifty largest metropolitan areas on these measures between 1990 and 2000. The region has a relatively large African American population, ranking fifteenth among the fifty largest metropolitan areas. However, compared with other large metro areas, job opportunities for African Americans are limited. St. Louis ranks ninth in black male unemployment (cf. Joiner 2005).

# St. Louis and the "New Economy"

One might fault these measures of economic and social vitality and growth as being too traditional, too much a part of the "old" industrial U.S. economy. How does the region perform on the so-called new economy indicators of knowledge, high-tech, and export-oriented jobs? For the most part, no better than on the traditional measures. The St. Louis region ranks thirty-seventh among the fifty largest metro areas in the percentage of the labor force in managerial, professional, or technical jobs and forty-first in manufacturing export sales per manufacturing worker, a measure of involvement in the global economy. St. Louis performs little better on such measures of economic dynamism as new public stock offerings (IPOs) as a share of gross metropolitan product (twenty-ninth) or measures of innovation such as new patents per worker (thirtieth)

---

[2] Author's calculations from the FBI's Uniform Crime Reports, retrieved from http://www.fbi.gov/ucr/cius_04/.

(Atkinson and Gottlieb 2001). However, hidden among the "new economy" indicators is one on which St. Louis ranks much higher: industry investment in academic research and total academic R&D.

St. Louis is sixth among the largest metro areas on this latent indicator of economic growth, just behind Salt Lake City, Washington, Austin, and Boston (Raleigh-Durham, which ranks first, is well ahead of the pack). St. Louis is not normally found in such august metropolitan company. Whether St. Louis's relatively large investment in academic research can be mobilized for future growth remains to be seen. In their contribution to this volume, Nasser Arshadi, Harvey A. Harris, and Thomas F. George discuss the potential of "technology transfer" from scientific discoveries to commercialized products to stimulate economic development in the St. Louis region.

# St. Louis and Its Midwestern Competitors

The nation's largest metropolitan areas may not constitute an appropriate base of comparison for assessing either St. Louis's present condition or its future development. How realistic or meaningful is it to compare St. Louis with a large coastal metropolis such as Los Angeles, San Francisco, or New York, or even with the midwestern behemoth Chicago, with its population of over nine million? Such comparisons are likely to make St. Louis's legendary "inferiority complex" worse than it already is (Schnuck 2005). No one realistically expects St. Louis to regain its status as the nation's fourth-largest city or to become a major global media or commercial center. The more pertinent question, at least for considering growth and development measured in decades rather than centuries, is how St. Louis stacks up against comparably sized metropolitan areas in the Midwest. Employers looking to relocate or expand are likely to narrow their focus on a particular region of the country and, within regions, on areas of about the same size.[3] Job seekers also have preferences about where they want or can afford to live. The St. Louis Regional Chamber and Growth Association's (RCGA) slogan for its current marketing

---

[3] A consultant hired by the Regional Chamber and Growth Association observed: "St. Louis firms, for the most part, find their most acute competition not from 'cool' cities on the coasts, but from faster-growing communities in the same general part of the country" (Kotkin 2004, 4).

campaign highlights St. Louis's location in the nation's midsection: "St!Louɪs: Perfectly Centered. Remarkably Connected." So, let us consider the employer or job seeker who already has decided to move to or remain in the Midwest and now must choose among several comparably sized metro areas. Based on the standard measures of growth and opportunity, how does St. Louis compare with its midwestern metropolitan competitors?

Table 1 compares St. Louis to Kansas City, Indianapolis, Cincinnati, and Minneapolis on selected census measures of income, employment, education, and population diversity. Other areas might have been selected for comparison, but these four offer a reasonable basis for assessing St. Louis's competitive prospects among comparable midwestern metro areas. The table presents each area's levels on the measures in 2000 and the percentage change in levels since 1990.

**Table 1. Five-Area Comparison on Selected Vitality and Growth Indicators**

|                     | St. Louis | Kansas City | Indianapolis | Cincinnati | Minneapolis |
|---------------------|-----------|-------------|--------------|------------|-------------|
| **Population**      |           |             |              |            |             |
| 2000                | 2,603,607 | 1,776,062   | 1,607,486    | 1,979,202  | 2,968,806   |
| 1990–2000 % change  | 6.53      | 13.39       | 28.62        | 13.48      | 20.48       |
| **Median Income**   |           |             |              |            |             |
| 2000                | 44,437    | 46,193      | 45,548       | 51,046     | 54,304      |
| 1990–2000 % change  | 39.85     | 46.12       | 43.89        | 64.79      | 48.51       |
| **% College**       |           |             |              |            |             |
| 2000                | 25.33     | 28.5        | 25.83        | 25.02      | 33.26       |
| 1990–2000 % change  | 22.19     | 21.99       | 22.42        | 23.71      | 22.59       |
| **% Poor**          |           |             |              |            |             |
| 2000                | 9.95      | 8.47        | 8.57         | 10.50      | 6.71        |
| 1990–2000 % change  | -7.51     | -13.68      | -10.7        | -7.21      | -16.94      |
| **% Unemployed**    |           |             |              |            |             |
| 2000                | 5.51      | 4.27        | 4.39         | 6.26       | 3.50        |
| 1990–2000 % change  | -13.55    | -21.96      | -7.45        | 21.05      | -23.84      |
| **% Black**         |           |             |              |            |             |
| 2000                | 18.31     | 12.75       | 13.93        | 11.67      | 5.32        |
| 1990–2000 % change  | 5.75      | -0.38       | 1.05         | -0.02      | 46.15       |
| **% Hispanic**      |           |             |              |            |             |
| 2000                | 1.52      | 5.23        | 2.67         | 1.14       | 3.34        |
| 1990–2000 % change  | 43.18     | 81.17       | 201.59       | 111.36     | 119.69      |
| **% Immigration***  |           |             |              |            |             |
| 2000                | 1.44      | 1.90        | 1.57         | 3.73       | 2.37        |
| 1990–2000 % change  | 73.21     | 102.04      | 131.61       | 553.13     | 94.1        |

Source: Appendix; U.S. Bureau of the Census.

* Percentage of population residing outside of the U.S. (excluding Puerto Rico) five years before.

St. Louis's population is larger than those of the other areas, with the exception of Minneapolis, which had about 370,000 more residents in 2000. However, St. Louis's growth during the previous decade did not keep pace with the increases registered in the other four areas. St. Louis grew at about one-half of the rate of Kansas City and Cincinnati, one-third of the rate of Minneapolis, and less than a quarter of Indianapolis's 29 percent growth rate. Census estimates for 2003 show additional population growth since 2000 in each of the five areas, but St. Louis continues to trail the others (U.S. Census Bureau 2005).

St. Louis's median household income of $44,437 in 2000 is the lowest among the five midwestern areas, and, more troubling still, its income growth over the previous ten years lagged behind that of the other areas. About one-quarter of the population age twenty-five and over in St. Louis, Indianapolis, and Cincinnati has a college degree, a slightly lower percentage than in Kansas City, and well below that in Minneapolis, where fully one-third of adults have a bachelor's or higher degree, a reflection of the large population of graduate students at the University of Minnesota. The college-educated population of all five metro areas grew at about the same rate between 1990 and 2000.

St. Louis has the second-highest poverty rate of the five areas, slightly below Cincinnati. The poverty rate dropped between 1990 and 2000 in all five of the areas, as it did elsewhere in the United States during the "roaring '90s," but poverty declined more slowly in St. Louis and Cincinnati than in the other midwestern areas. The same is true of unemployment: St. Louis's unemployment rate is higher than the unemployment rates of the other areas, with the exception of Cincinnati's, and unemployment fell more slowly in St. Louis than in three of the four comparison areas since 1990.

St. Louis's position on these well-being and growth indicators relative to other midwestern metro areas is similar to its relative position at the national level. To the extent that businesses and individuals rely on such measures for deciding where to move, St. Louis is not an attractive alternative to Kansas City, Indianapolis, or Minneapolis. On the economic distress measures of poverty and unemployment, it's a toss-up between St. Louis and Cincinnati. Nor does St. Louis compare favorably to its midwestern competitors on the so-called new economy performance standards.

Immigrants evidently do use such measures for choosing a destination within the United States, because the percentage of the St. Louis population that resided outside of the country five years earlier is lower and its population of new immigrants grew less rapidly than in the other areas. With the exception of Cincinnati, St. Louis also has the smallest Hispanic proportion of the population and a slower growth rate among Hispanics than all four of the comparison areas. St. Louis does have a larger African American population than the other metro areas, and it grew faster between 1990 and 2000 than in the other areas, with the exception of Minneapolis's relatively small African American population, which increased by nearly one-half during the 1990s.

It is difficult to say how attractive St. Louis is for African Americans in comparison to other midwestern metro areas. On the one hand, a comparatively large African American population is likely to be a draw for additional African American in-migration. On the other hand, economic opportunities for African Americans look better elsewhere in the Midwest. Among the four comparison areas, only Cincinnati has a higher rate of unemployment among black males than St. Louis. But that mirrors the unemployment situation generally among the five midwestern metro areas. One commentator maintains that "shoring up our economy" is the first priority in stemming the "brain drain" of upwardly mobile African Americans from the St. Louis area (Joiner 2005). As difficult as that will be, it may take even more to retain and attract young African Americans who have the opportunity to live and work in other places. St. Louis neighborhoods remain highly segregated by race, more segregated than three of the four midwestern comparison areas, with Cincinnati again being the exception (Social Science Data Analysis Network 2005). Because African Americans have strong preferences for living in racially integrated neighborhoods (Farley, Fielding, and Krysan 1997), the brain drain is likely to continue absent visible progress in reducing racial segregation.

# Connecting the Past to the Future

Our hypothetical employer or job seeker who relies solely on the standard performance measures in deciding whether to move to or remain in St. Louis is likely to locate elsewhere in the Midwest. African Americans or anyone with a strong preference to live in a racially integrated community may have additional reasons to prefer Kansas City, Indianapolis, or

Minneapolis over St. Louis. This is not good news for St. Louis, but neither is it the whole story of the region's prospects.

First, St. Louis is not at the bottom of the nation's metro areas on any of the standard performance measures; although the region struggles in comparison to other midwestern cities, nationally St. Louis falls in the middle of the distribution on most of the performance measures, and it has held this ranking for some time.

Second, metropolitan growth is not always or necessarily a zero-sum game in which one area's gain is another's loss. Most areas of the country benefit from periods of sustained national economic growth, such as during the 1990s, even if some grow more rapidly than others. Incomes and educational attainment rose, and poverty and unemployment fell in St. Louis between 1990 and 2000. Other areas may have benefited more from the 1990s economic boom, but on average St. Louis residents were better off at the end of the decade than at the beginning.

Finally, and most pertinent to this volume, the standard measures do not exhaust the qualities that make a community valuable to its residents and attractive to non-residents. St. Louis clearly has a great many of these qualities, as the following pages document. These hidden assets—rivers, parks, architecture, housing, sports, music, research investments, and others—should not be thought of as alternatives to economic opportunity or growth. On the contrary, they are essential preconditions for future growth and development in the region. If they are to generate growth, they must be "promoted," but at the same time they must be handled in the way of a well-tended garden, with patience, intelligence, and day-to-day nurturing. St. Louis can be competitive with other metro areas for people and business only if it harnesses its persisting market advantages and distinctive history to its plans and initiatives for growth.

St. Louis's persisting market advantage is its *affordability*, a product of its midwestern location and, ironically, its relatively slow growth. St. Louis ranks second among the fifty largest metro areas in housing affordability and sixteenth in overall cost of living (*St. Louis Business Journal* 2005). The region's main hidden asset is its *quality of life*, a product of its distinctive history. The irony of course is that, to the extent that campaigns to promote growth are successful, they risk undermining the very condition— affordable quality of life—that attracts people and business to the region. However, in light of St. Louis's modest track record in promoting growth and its enormous capacity to absorb additional growth without running up against natural or artificial barriers, that is a risk well worth taking.

It is useful to partition the somewhat nebulous idea of metropolitan "growth" into two types: distinctive and generic. Distinctive patterns of growth derive from, make use of, and replenish an area's specific assets, especially those that distinguish it from other areas. Generic growth is unrelated to an area's distinctive and valuable qualities and, unimpeded, may damage them. Runaway suburban and exurban sprawl that adds to traffic congestion, increases commute times, and multiplies look-alike housing tracts and shopping facilities is an example of generic growth that neither uses nor safeguards St. Louis's precious assets. "Growth" of this kind (assuming net increases to the region in people and business) can and does occur everywhere. Land is relatively cheap on the outskirts of most midwestern metropolitan areas, and St. Louis has no obvious advantages over Kansas City or Indianapolis in subdividing farmland for residential or commercial development. Generic growth entails competition mainly on the basis of price, and although the cost of living in St. Louis is low by national standards, it is not appreciably lower than in other midwestern metro areas.

Distinctive growth patterns are channeled through an area's special assets. Good examples include the resurgence of the "Loop" district and the Soulard neighborhood, rehabilitated homes in the Tower Grove and Benton Park neighborhoods, and the frenetic conversion of downtown warehouses into lofts, restaurants, galleries, and nightclubs (Ferriss 2005; St. Louis Post-Dispatch 2005). In each instance, development depends on existing assets (older brick homes, beautiful parks, cobblestone streets, architecturally distinctive buildings) and replenishes them. Distinctive growth is often unanticipated, at least in the beginning stages, and usually occurs in fits and starts. The expansion of the Loop entertainment district was not part of an official development "plan," nor were the downtown lofts. But once begun, distinctive growth can be nurtured and spin-offs designed, as in the case of the "Bottle District" shops, restaurants, and new housing under construction in downtown St. Louis (St. Louis Post-Dispatch 2005). Some distinctive growth does result from formal planning, such as the major restoration in the midtown area and the new construction around the Botanical Garden. Planned or unplanned, distinctive growth merits significant public and private investment, not simply because it is "good for the community," but also because it is likely to yield higher and more sustained economic returns to the region than the copycat generic growth common everywhere.

The best marketing, it is said, is niche marketing. St. Louis's many and overlapping hidden assets constitute the niche within which its marketing efforts should be concentrated. The RCGA's current marketing campaign rightly trumpets the image of St. Louis as a big-city environment with the "availability," "accessibility," and "sanity" of smaller communities (St. Louis RCGA 2005). It is the *combination* of big-city amenities with the affordability and comforts of smaller locales that sets St. Louis apart from its midwestern metropolitan competitors. Comfort, convenience, and midwestern values do not qualitatively distinguish St. Louis from Kansas City, Indianapolis, Cincinnati, or Minneapolis. Its history does. St. Louis was once the nation's fourth-largest city, and even as its national stature has diminished, it has retained the traditions, amenities, and economic and cultural diversity of a great city. Understandably, perhaps, marketing campaigns do not focus on St. Louis's past. Nonetheless, many of the region's hidden assets—the parks, red brick homes, sports, music, neighborhood traditions, and river commerce—have deep historical roots. More than most places, the region's future depends on its past.

St. Louis has three possible futures: (1) stasis—the region retains pockets of strength but does not grow or develop in desirable ways; (2) decay—St. Louis declines economically and loses population, pulled down by an increasingly impoverished inner core; (3) non-obvious development—the present hidden assets interact and multiply. The commercial and entertainment districts continue to expand; new ones sprout. The plant sciences continue to grow in new commercially viable biotechnology ventures. Beautiful brick homes throughout the central city and suburbs attract rehab developers and buyers. The music scene generates production facilities, enticing recording companies to relocate. Light-rail expands. The trick is to nurture continued sustainable growth in the package of hidden assets. Such developments may not, at least in the near future, register on the standard indicators of metropolitan vitality and growth. But they represent an attractive alternative future to stasis or decay.

# References

Atkinson, Robert D., and Paul D. Gottlieb. *The Metropolitan New Economy Index*. Washington, DC: Progressive Policy Institute, 2001. http://www.neweconomyindex.org/metro/index.html.

Department of Justice, Federal Bureau of Investigation. "Crime in the United States, 2004." http://www.fbi.gov/ucr/cius_04/.

Farley, Reynolds, Elaine L. Fielding, and Maria Krysan. "The Residential Preferences of Blacks and Whites: A Four Metropolis Analysis." *Housing Policy Debate* 8 (1997): 763–800.

Ferriss, Lucy. "St. Louis: Old Warehouses, New Promise." *New York Times*, October 2, 2005, travel section, p. 4.

Joiner, Robert. "The Black Flight and Brain Drain." *St. Louis Post-Dispatch*, August 8, 2005, p. B7.

Kotkin, Joel. *The Corps of Rediscovery: St. Louis in the 21st Century*. St. Louis: St. Louis Regional Chamber and Growth Association, 2004.

Schnuck, Scott C. "Everyone Will Benefit from New Businesses and New Jobs. But We Have to Shed, Once and for All, Our Inferiority Complex." *St. Louis Post-Dispatch*, November 2, 2005, p. C11.

Social Science Data Analysis Network. "CensusScope: Racial Segregation Statistics for Cities and Metropolitan Areas," 2005. http://www.censusscope.org/segregation.html.

*St. Louis Business Journal*. "St. Louis's Housing Affordability No. 2 Among Major Metro Areas," January 7, 2005. http://www.bizjournals.com/stlouis/stories/2005/01/03/daily70.html.

*St. Louis Post-Dispatch*. "Downtown: The View from Here Gets Better Everyday," October 5, 2005, p. B6.

St. Louis Regional Chamber and Growth Association. "Regional and County Profiles: Greater St. Louis Area," 2005. http://www.stlrcga.org/.

U.S. Census Bureau. *Statistical Abstract of the United States: Population*. Washington, DC: U.S. Government Printing Office, 2005. http://www.census.gov/prod/2004pubs/04statab/pop.pdf.

# Chapter 1

# Other Arches, Other Gateways

## Robert W. Duffy

Let us not be naive about St. Louis's architectural hidden assets. Some are not merely inconspicuous, they are also quite permanently gone, reduced to rubble by wreckers or stripped of their fancy parts to be sold in antiques establishments, then demolished (Toft and Josse 2002).

Our store of built assets in St. Louis, hidden and not so, has been ransacked in too many places, leaving gaps and cavities and shards on the floor. For those who are open to the rich and varied language of architecture and to its spiritual presence, a profound sense of loss is felt when they survey the cityscape.

Sometimes the losses make folks angry. Once such case was the needless demolition of the Century Building at Ninth and Olive streets downtown. The 108-year-old building was razed in order to build a parking garage. Ironically, the National Trust for Historic Preservation provided New Markets Tax Credits to help to pay for a renovation of the Old Post Office across the street from the Century. The developers of the post office project claimed their project could not succeed without adjacent parking. The City of St. Louis and the State of Missouri supported their position (Duffy 2004). So the Century Building is gone, and it joins a venerable group of St. Louis edifices in Vishwakarma's[1] graveyard.

In fact, a host of buildings in that architectural cemetery once stood sturdily on the ground where the steely majesty of Eero Saarinen's Gateway Arch stands today. As many as forty square blocks of eighteenth- and nineteenth-century buildings fell to make room for the Jefferson National Expansion Memorial, which includes the Arch. While we stand in awe of the product of Saarinen's genius, the civic jury hangs back, debating still the question of whether we should have effected this massive clearance and others in the city's core in the mid-twentieth century.

---

[1] Vishwakarma is the deity of all architects.

**View looking southeast toward the Old Courthouse and the Gateway Arch. Photograph by Joseph Vohsen, 1971. MHS Photographs and Prints.**

Far, far too many of our assets have been squandered for purposes far less consequential than the building of a great, monumental work of art that has become a regional and a national symbol. In 2005 the radiant Busch Stadium fell to be replaced by an anodyne commercial playground; the only solid reason for this vandalism was money (Duffy 2003).

The barbarians have been inside the gates so long now they have gained respectability and will continue to propel their headache balls for reasons of vanity, whimsy, and concupiscence. The purpose of this book is to offer—without the veil of naiveté—a reminder that much remains of the fine tapestry that is our regional material history and heritage. This collection of assets is sometimes unavoidably apparent, sometimes demure, sometimes unappreciated.

The weaving of it began in prehistory, and the shuttle continues to be shot from side to side. Although threads have been yanked from this tapestry, and the wasting effects of time have worn parts of it away, what remains is regularly found to be resplendent or, in its unadorned simplicity, to be an extraordinary revelation of the truth of Ludwig Mies Van Der Rohe's observation of less being more.

Before the second half of the twentieth century, when the civic establishment and the local architects it supports came under the sway of postmodernism and historicism (see the Federal Courthouse and the new Busch Stadium for egregious examples), St. Louis maintained extraordinarily high standards for its built environment. Architects and firms such as H. H. Richardson; Shepley, Rutan and Coolidge; Louis Henri Sullivan, and others brought their talents to the building of our great architectural treasury. Local firms such as Eames and Young; Mauran, Russell and Crowell; and Jamieson and Spearl all made valuable contributions, as did generations of architects named Barnett. Theodore Link's Union Station, which almost did not survive, remains as a triumph of design and civic substance. Link's Second Presbyterian Church in the Central West End is a masterpiece of ecclesiastical design and was inspired in part by Richardson's Trinity Church in Boston (McCue and Peters 1989).

Others followed in the modernist tradition that developed in the early years of the twentieth century in Europe. Some of the names of local architects that still resonate are Harris Armstrong, Edouard Mutrux and William Adair Bernoudy, Eugene Mackey *père et fils*, Frederick Dunn, Charles Nagel, Ralph Cole Hall and design collaborator Victor Proetz, the firm of Hellmuth, Obata and Kassabaum in its early days, the firm of Powers Bowersox recently, and the Cannon firm following the leadership of George Nicholajevich.

Masters with national and international reputations who designed buildings here include Eric Mendelsohn, Minoru Yamasaki, Fumihiko Maki, Philip Johnson, Edward Larabee Barnes, Edward Durell Stone, and the recent national sensation Brad Cloepfil.

Names of many worthy men and women have been omitted, not because of any inadequacy necessarily, but simply to prevent this from becoming a laundry list. Nevertheless, the substance to which all of them contributed is so visible and so impressive visitors often tell St. Louisans how fortunate we are to have so many magnificent buildings standing. "You had something to start with when you began to revive your downtown," a new arrival said recently.

The genesis is prehistoric. To experience it all you have to do is to travel about twenty minutes into Illinois from the Arch grounds and visit the monumental earthworks created by the Mississippian people before Europeans showed up in this region. The remains of this complex culture are on Collinsville Road south of I-70 (McCue and Peters 1989). This culture, and related ones, existed for a thousand years in what is now the eastern United States and flourished abundantly in this region before the fifteenth century. Then it vanished from the face of the earth as if it had been absorbed into it (Sharp 2004).

Nevertheless, the Mississippians left behind haunting material testimony to their brilliance as builders, farmers, scientists, artists, craftspeople, and governors. An exhibition called *Hero, Hawk, and Open Hand: American Indian Art of the Ancient Midwest and South* at the Art Institute of Chicago and the Saint Louis Art Museum in 2004–2005 gave eloquent testimony to their aesthetic powers and visual acuity (Sharp 2004).

**Big Mound. Fifth and Mound streets, St. Louis. Daguerreotype by Thomas M. Easterly, ca. 1852–1854. Photograph by David Schultz, 1994. MHS Photographs and Prints.**

In 2000, *St. Louis Post-Dispatch* reporters William Allen and John G. Carlton wrote a fascinating account of prehistoric life here. They reported the perceptions of archaeologist F. Terry Norris, who—when he surveyed the trash-strewn, weed-choked wasteland just north of the Laclede's Landing neighborhood on the riverbank—noted this had been near to the center of a "city defined by two dozen earthen pyramids that lent St. Louis its early nickname among white settlers: Mound City" (Allen and Carlton 2000). Progress annihilated these mounds. One remains on the western

Hidden Assets

shore of the Mississippi—a partial mound with a house built on top of it, visible from Highway 55 just south of downtown.

Interestingly, astonishingly perhaps, little remains of the eighteenth- or early nineteenth-century village of St. Louis, and nothing remains of the town known to Meriwether Lewis and William Clark, who arrived here in 1803 on their way to the Pacific through the Louisiana Territory.

One very hidden asset is the remains of a stone building in the Lafayette Square neighborhood, just south of the old Edge restaurant on Missouri Avenue and LaSalle Street. It may have been around when the explorers arrived, but the valiant Landmarks Association of St. Louis has been able to trace it back only to the 1830s or 1840s. It is an interesting ruin nevertheless. While other scattered remnants may remain, nothing of colonial St. Louis exists downtown other than its grid.[2]

There are good places just beyond the mighty shadows and reflections of the Arch to see buildings of the eighteenth and early nineteenth centuries, however. One is the town of Cahokia, Illinois. Settled in 1699 and distinct from the mounds site, it is southeast of downtown St. Louis. Among the period buildings there are the restored Church of the Holy Family, the rebuilt Cahokia Courthouse, and a house built in 1810 by Nicholas Jarrot, a landowner and businessman, considered the oldest brick building in Illinois (McCue and Peters 1989).

Florissant, in north St. Louis County, is the largest independent municipality in St. Louis County. It too boasts architectural remains of the eighteenth and nineteenth centuries—the 1790 Casa Alvarez, for example—and the names of streets in the town center are unmistakable reminders of the French heritage of the region (McCue and Peters 1989).

The graceful town of Ste. Genevieve, about sixty-five miles south of St. Louis, has a number of eighteenth- and nineteenth-century buildings in excellent states of preservation. In the mid-twentieth century, Ste. Genevieve also was home to a colony of regional artists who found the village a hospitable place to work (Duffy 1998).

And if you wander around the countryside south and southwest of St. Louis, you often stumble across the spare, eloquent buildings that speak a French–New World patois.

As rich and admirable as all this may be, the buildings that form our most prepossessing heritage and that are likely to have enduring meaning are those that rose during the dynamic century between the middle of the nineteenth century and 1950, when the urban fabric began to fray in dangerous and random ways.

---

[2] Carolyn Toft, interview by Robert Duffy, 2003, St. Louis, Missouri.

It is a good idea to look across the river from the Arch to East St. Louis to see just how rapidly an urban cataclysm can occur. For many, clear memories exist of East St. Louis as a prosperous, middle-class city, not without problems, but vital nevertheless. To visit there today is to find a raggedy city. One of the most satisfying ways to return to the western bank of the Mississippi is to cross via the Eads Bridge, which in the nineteenth century was as much a brilliant concatenation of art, engineering, and symbol as its twentieth-century neighbor the Gateway Arch.

This bridge, from 1874, is among the great spans of the world, and its inventor and builder, Captain James Buchanan Eads, is one of the nineteenth century's most fascinating and complex individuals. His bridge is an asset that begs to be explored and to be more thoroughly used. Its great stone arches on the riverbank that hearken back to Rome, the graceful flow of the revolutionary steel arches that carry the railroad and vehicular beds, the magnificent vistas it offers—all conspire to make it a place of magic and inspiration. Walt Whitman wrote of it in 1879, "I have haunted the river every night lately, where I could get a look at the bridge by moonlight. It is indeed a structure of perfection and beauty unsurpassable, and I never tire of it" (Whitman 2004).

**Eads Bridge and the St. Louis skyline from the Illinois shore. Photograph by Glenn S. Hensley, 1984. MHS Photographs and Prints.**

There are places such as the Eads Bridge that should be seen in the region if one is to appreciate St. Louis's built assets and to come away with a sense of affirmation and a sense of possibility. For example, as you reach the western shore of the river on the Eads Bridge, you see the Arch on your left, and on your right is an ensemble of buildings called Laclede's Landing that stand today not only as a reminder of the robust commercialism and vigorous and varied architecture of nineteenth-century St. Louis but also as a testament to a commitment to historic preservation that took hold in the 1970s and—although scorned and mocked at times—has remained a dynamic and independent force in the community.

Eads Bridge evolves into Washington Avenue when it connects with St. Louis. On the north side of Washington at Fourth Street is the Missouri Athletic Club, designed by William B. Ittner. Although Ittner was certainly not opposed to work supplied by social aspirants who wished to exclude themselves from the hoi polloi, such as this men's club, his greatest achievements are his public school buildings, which are to be found all over St. Louis—and all over the United States. Open, light filled, welcoming, and generously accented with decorative art inside and out, these buildings stand separately and together as genuinely noble achievements and give St. Louis special distinction for their innovative qualities and their quiet dignity. Some continue to perform their original work as schoolhouses. Others are finding new life as residential buildings. We are lucky to have them (*St. Louis Post-Dispatch* 2004).

Travel west on Washington and you get a sense of the dynamism of St. Louis between 1850 and 1950, where broad-shouldered commercial buildings, now finding new life as loft dwellings, create a vast urban canyon of light and shadow, masonry and brick, and are animated by an ever-growing human parade. Washington Avenue was home to St. Louis's shoemaking and garment industries, and a hundred years ago was a dense, bustling, prosperous center of manufacturing. At the turn of the twenty-first century, it was looking down at the heels. A strong planning effort brought it back as an entertainment, convention, and residential district.

**Washington Avenue west from Tenth Street (Wholesale District).
Photograph by George Stark, 1903. MHS Photographs and Prints.**

A few blocks south of Washington, at Seventh and Chestnut, stands the Wainwright Building, considered the prototype of the modern skyscraper because of the frank articulation of its steel-frame construction. Captain Eads inspired its architect, the Chicago-school pillar Louis Henri Sullivan, among other great builders (Scott 1979). The Wainwright, preserved by the State of Missouri as an office building, is a prominent asset, a landmark on any international architectural pilgrimage (McCue and Peters 1989).

To walk around downtown St. Louis is to discover a catalog of hidden assets—buildings that reveal a respect for human scale but have no hesitation to take pleasure in the variety of shapes and forms that give architecture its wildly diverse beauty. Washington Avenue offers not only the grandeur of the nineteenth century but also farther out, past Grand Boulevard, another building whose exterior modesty conceals an astonishingly moving interior.

This is the Pulitzer Foundation for the Arts in Grand Center. Designed by the Japanese architect Tadao Ando and completed in 2001, the structure's austere face belies a building of openness, light, and serenity, where exhibitions are carefully designed to involve themselves with the building's character.

**Wainwright Building. Photograph by Emil Boehl, ca. 1907.
MHS Photographs and Prints.**

The Eads Bridge, the Arch, the Wainwright Building, and the Pulitzer building form a quartet of structures as great as any in the world. They testify to the power of progressivism in design, rather than the current craze for retrospection.

As remarkable as these landmarks are, St. Louis's more modest offerings are in their way equally affecting to those of us who live here and to visitors alike. Anyone can gain perspective on a city by allowing himself or herself to deliberately get lost in it, and that is my recommendation when experiencing St. Louis.

Valuable lessons in the visual and transformative powers of architecture come from explorations of modest nineteenth-century neighborhoods in north and south St. Louis where the fabric is mercifully intact, where there once existed a sensible relationship of home and workplace, reducing the need for expensive, resource-guzzling transportation.

In the central corridor, as one moves east to west, one passes from the mercantilism and commerce to the grandeur and magnificence of the Central West End. Beyond, south, east, and west, are the suburbs, which offer a textbook example of urban growth, good and bad. But everywhere, from the Cahokia Mounds to far suburbia, there are buildings and carefully planned landscapes and parks that recommend themselves to residents and visitors.

One eerily magnificent place to visit is one of America's finest necropolises, Bellefontaine Cemetery, where the tastes and social structure of the region are laid out with astonishing clarity. Then, in the south, on a hill near the old village of Carondelet, which is home to some of the oldest existing buildings in the region, there is a small, inconspicuous park called Bellerive, a hidden asset where travelers through time, space, architecture, and life are welcome to sit in relative isolation and reflect upon a city's past and puzzle its future, while before them the strong brown god rolls inexorably down to the sea.

Consider with me why St. Louis, so conservative in so many ways, developed an architecture of genuine quality from the mid-nineteenth to the mid-twentieth century—the architecture that continues to enrich the lives of those who live here and those who come to call on us. There are several strands in the braid that is the history of St. Louis. The French brought a cosmopolitanism and sophistication to the region; the English and Scots a commercial canniness and a taste for danger; the Germans and Jews a deep respect for art and learning. None of these generalizations is 100 percent accurate of course.

Each group, and all of those who have followed, made distinct contributions and similar contributions. The commingling, while not altogether inclusive, worked in the nineteenth century to create a progressive community that built buildings that were—are—worldly and optimistic.

I deliberately got lost recently in a neighborhood in the vicinity of two of St. Louis's broad avenues—Jefferson and Gravois. The experience was astonishing. I had been there before, but I had never been there before as a visual explorer, a person who was able to slow down and to let my eyes wander across the faces of buildings that, while in many ways similar, have their own distinct characters and identities. I was discovering new territory. It was stimulating. It was St. Louis near the Arch, yet light-years beyond it.

### References

Allen, William, and John G. Carlton. "Much Evidence of Mississippian Culture Has Succumbed to Bulldozer and Plow." *St. Louis Post-Dispatch*, January 9, 2000, p. A6.

Duffy, Robert. "Century Building Dies Senseless Death Downtown." *St. Louis Post-Dispatch*, October 31, 2004, p. B1.

———. "Foundation Honors Historic Art Colony." *St. Louis Post-Dispatch*, October 11, 1998, p. C4.

———. "Retro Should Be a No Go for New Stadium." *St. Louis Post-Dispatch*, January 5, 2003, p. G3.

McCue, George, and Frank Peters. *A Guide to the Architecture of St. Louis*. Columbia: University of Missouri Press, 1989.

Scott, Quinta. *The Eads Bridge*. Historical appraisal by Howard S. Miller. Columbia: University of Missouri Press, 1979.

Sharp, Robert V., ed. *Hero, Hawk, and Open Hand: American Indian Art of the Ancient Midwest and South*. Chicago: Art Institute of Chicago, 2004.

*St. Louis Post-Dispatch*. "Condos with History: Ittner Architectural Gem Gives Home School New Meaning," May 5, 2004, p. B1.

Toft, Carolyn Hewes. *St. Louis: Landmarks and Historic Districts*. With Lynn Josse. St. Louis: Landmarks Association of St. Louis Inc., 2002.

Whitman, Walt. "Specimen Days and Collect." In *The Portable Walt Whitman*, edited by Michael Warner. New York: Penguin Classics, 2004.

# Chapter 2
# St. Louis and the Automobile

## Thomas H. Eyssell

St. Louis, already an undisputed shipping center, was growing into one of the country's premier automotive centers. . . . By 1930, St. Louis was, or had been, home to dozens of automobile manufacturers, who produced such makes as Dorris, Gardner, St. Louis, and Victor cars; Eureka and Success motor buggies; Darby, Eagle, and Traffic trucks; and Robinson and Webb fire engines. —*Curt McConnell*, Great Cars of the Great Plains, *1995*

"Village Blacksmith to Run Filling Station"
Barney Clark, who has been the blacksmith in what was once the village of Winstanley but which is now part of East St. Louis, has watched his business diminish until he can no longer earn a living. Yesterday he made application to City Commissioner Michael J. Whalen for a license to open an oil and filling station on the site of his shop on State street, between Twenty-fifth and Twenty-sixth streets. —St. Louis Globe-Democrat, *June 16, 1925*

The role played by St. Louis in the early development and manufacture of the automobile is important but, unfortunately, not well known. Histories of the domestic automobile industry tend to focus on developments in the northeastern United States, in Ohio, and, of course, in Detroit—few, however, take note of St. Louis's importance. Perhaps it is because Detroit overshadows everything else, or perhaps it is because some of the most famous marques produced in St. Louis disappeared before the beginning of World War II. Whatever the reason, this history is one of St. Louis's hidden assets and deserves to be told.

The economic repercussions of decisions made decades ago continue to this day. According to a recent *St. Louis Post-Dispatch* article, approximately ten thousand Missourians are employed directly in automobile assembly plants, and half again as many are employed by suppliers (Nicklaus 2004). Missouri governor Matt Blunt has led a group of state officials to Detroit. In the words of one official: "The whole intent of the group is to show the Big Three automakers that the St. Louis region is solidly behind auto manufacturers. This [region] is a model; there's nothing like it in the United States."

St. Louis's role in this story also tantalizes the reader as a fascinating example of what might have been—yet another example of the "woulda-coulda-shoulda" events that seem to characterize the city's history. There are those who claim that, but for a few twists of fate, St. Louis, not Detroit, would have been the center of global automobile production throughout the twentieth century. While this may overstate the case a bit, it is clear that St. Louis was home to some of history's important early manufacturers, the home of the first automobile supply house in the country, and the home of the first gasoline station in the country. Most important, the St. Louis region was responsible for the largest volume of automobile production in the country for several decades, outside of Detroit.

# In the Beginning: Years of Growth

There is hardly an inventor of any prominence who is not more or less engaged in perfecting the automobile. At the Patent Office in Washington the applications for patents on different parts of the automobile are so numerous that it exceeds the activity which existed when the bicycle began to make its appearance in general use.—The Horseless Age, *June 27, 1900*

Few inventions have had more impact on Western civilization than the automobile. The automobile has facilitated the movement from farm to city and from city to suburb, and is more pervasive in the United States than anywhere else on earth. A recent study of automobile ownership indicated that there are about nine hundred vehicles for every thousand citizens of the United States, about twice the proportion of Europe and nearly ten times that of China. Automobile manufacturing played a key role in the growth of union power through the mid-twentieth century and has spawned numerous related industries—suppliers, petroleum, highways, etc. Indeed, it is difficult to overstate the economic and social importance of this invention; it is estimated that one in six workers in America is employed in an automobile-related industry.

John Rae suggests that the automobile industry "embodies the characteristics in which Americans like to believe that they excel: inventive genius, technological 'know-how,' and organizing ability." Perhaps the ubiquity of these characteristics is exemplified by the large number of tinkerers, shade tree mechanics, and budding industrialists who were building "horseless carriages" and "auto-buggies" in sheds, barns, and garages across the country in the 1890s (Rae 1959). Whatever the reason, the dawn of the twentieth century witnessed a boom of entrants into automobile production. Consider this statement from an early enthusiast publication: "The formation of automobile companies has been so frequent lately that the announcement attracts no attention now . . . the number of such companies having a corporate existence under the laws of New Jersey, Delaware, West Virginia and other charter-making States, is considerably over 500. . . . In addition to the large number of concerns, of which there is a state record, there is a still larger number which exist as copartnerships or firms" (*The Horseless Age* 1900, 25).

Of course, only a fraction of these firms ever reached the point of actually producing a single prototype vehicle, let alone manufacturing on a large scale.[1] Nonetheless, it is not surprising that the twentieth century has been called the "automobile century."

St. Louis firms played a key role in the development of the automobile industry for a period stretching from the late 1890s until industry consolidation and the Great Depression wiped out all but the hardiest automakers. Although estimates vary, it has been said that more than two hundred U.S. automakers disappeared between 1920 and 1935; a large

---

[1] "Manufacturing" is used here to denote the process of producing a completed vehicle—most of the automobile "manufacturers" of this era were actually "assemblers," i.e., they acquired components from various suppliers, assembled the vehicles, and then badged them as their own. Hochfelder and Helper (1996) note that "over a hundred car makers entered the market between roughly 1903 and 1918" and "nearly all assembled their automobiles from outsourced motors, transmissions, and chassis" (39). Similarly, Langlois and Robertson (1989) state that "virtually all automobile companies began as assemblers rather than manufacturers" (366). In-house manufacturing, or more precisely, vertical integration, in the automobile industry began in earnest only after the product market had begun to coalesce.

proportion of these failures can be attributed to severe economic times.[2] The impact of the Depression-related downturn in the automobile industry is indicated by the fact that production peaked at 5.3 million vehicles in 1929 and didn't again reach that level until 1948 (*Collier's Yearbook* 1949).

# Local Growth: St. Louis Becomes a Player

From a financial viewpoint, the automobile business, in its combined assembling and distributing phases, exceeds any other business activity in St. Louis.—*Lewis F. Thomas*, The Localization of Business Activities in Metropolitan St. Louis, *1927*

The St. Louis economy expanded rapidly in the latter half of the nineteenth century due in no small part to its central location and the existence of barge traffic, railroads, warehouses, and port facilities second only to those of New York City. Primm (1990) notes that "St. Louis's transportation facilities were unsurpassed elsewhere." This advantage was trumpeted by the city fathers of the era; a 1917 publication of the St. Louis Chamber of Commerce states: "The geographical location of St. Louis makes it a logical distributing point for automobiles for the West, Southwest, South, Central East and North. . . . Freight costs per automobile are lower to these districts than on shipments from Detroit, Cleveland or Indianapolis and the time of delivery is much shorter. The saving in freight is sufficient to give to the dealer practically an increased profit of five per cent" (McConnell 1995, 205).

Adding to its desirability, St. Louis's banking system had developed to the point that capital for business formation was readily available. Some

---

[2] The magnitude of shakeout and consolidation in the automobile industry is described by Thomas (1977) who comments on the fierce market conditions in the automobile industry during the early part of the twentieth century: "The penalty for an incorrect response to a changing competitive situation was often more serious than a change in management or temporary financial reverse. The continued existence of the firm was often called into question. This appears from the available statistics not to have been uncommon; of the more than 950 different concerns that tried to manufacture automobiles between 1896 and 1929, only twenty-three remained in the industry in 1929. The average life expectancy of an automobile firm was estimated by one student of the industry, to be less than six years" (5).

hint of this growing economic prominence is suggested by the fact that, in the competition among cities to be selected by the newly formed Federal Reserve System to host a regional Federal Reserve Bank, St. Louis was a key player. As Primm (1990, 38) notes:

> Would St. Louis have a Federal Reserve bank? Without a doubt, thought the city's bankers. It was the nation's fourth-largest city, and one of only three central reserve cities in the national banking system. With 26 trunk line railroads, it was a major hub of the mid-continent and southwestern distribution systems, and it led the nation in shipping hardware, hardwood lumber, and a variety of agricultural products. In manufacturing the city was a national leader in shoes, stoves, streetcars, and millinery.

Thus, with an industrial base in place, excellent transportation facilities, access to capital, and a large labor pool, it is not surprising that St. Louis was to become a key player in the rapidly developing automobile industry.

# Prewar Auto Manufacturing in St. Louis:
# St. Louis's "Big Three" and "Little Three"

The importance of St. Louis in the development and manufacture of the automobile can be broken rather neatly into two eras: prior to World War II, the city was home to several native automakers which produced distinctive vehicles but ultimately fell prey to economic reversals and growing industry competition. Three of these firms—Dorris, Gardner, and Moon—had lives measured in decades and produced relatively large numbers of vehicles. These firms and their products are fondly remembered by auto buffs, and will be referred to as St. Louis's "Big Three."

Of arguably equal importance, however, are a number of firms whose lives were generally shorter and did not produce many vehicles, but whose relevance stems from some pioneering aspect of their existence. St. Louis's "Little Three"—the St. Louis Motor Carriage Company, the St. Louis Car Company, and the St. Louis Automobile and Supply Company—all earned a place in St. Louis automotive history by paving the way, in one way or another, for those to come.

## St. Louis's "Big Three": Dorris, Gardner, and Moon

The Dorris Motor Car Company was the brainchild of George Preston Dorris and enjoyed relatively long-lived success by manufacturing automobiles primarily for the luxury market. George Dorris has been called "the pioneer automobile manufacturer in St. Louis" (Rae 1959, 38) due to his role in the founding of the St. Louis Motor Carriage Company, and later in the founding of Dorris Motor Car Company.

Dorris began his career as the chief engineer for the St. Louis Motor Carriage Company in 1899, for which he designed the firm's first vehicle. The firm's product line expanded, and sales grew rapidly. However, shortly after one of the firm's founders was killed, all operations were moved to Peoria, Illinois. Dorris elected to stay in St. Louis to found his own firm—the Dorris Motor Car Company.

The Dorris Motor Car Company debuted its first automobile at the 1906 New York Auto Show. Sales increased sufficiently that, by the late teens, the firm recapitalized as the Dorris Motors Corporation and issued 165,000 shares of common and preferred stock. At the same time, the firm acquired the Astra Motors Corporation and, according to the security issuance, expected earnings in 1920 of $1.3 million.

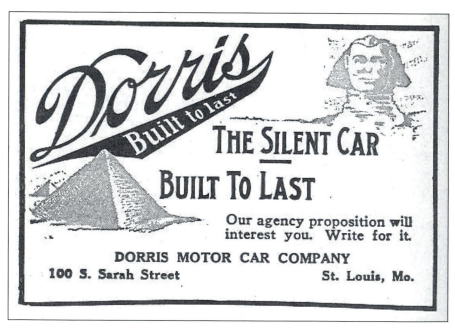

**Dorris Motor Car Company advertisement from**
*Motor Age,* **March 20, 1913. Collection of the author.**

Dorris cars were expensive and largely hand built, with production rates peaking at something over one vehicle per week. Advertised as "the most beautiful car in St. Louis," Dorris automobiles were of particularly high quality and priced accordingly. "Built to Last" and "Built Up to a Standard—Not Down to a Price" were the firm's slogans for many years. The 1922 Dorris Model 6-80 was described as follows: "Powered by a king-sized valve-in-head 'six,' the 1922 Dorris Model 6-80 was substantial in appearance as well as in construction. The wheelbase was 132 inches. Nickel-finish headlights and radiator shell were included, and there were two ventilators atop the hood (for cooling the engine) as well as the cowl vent" (Burgess 1968, 95).

Unfortunately, the automobile industry was evolving toward high-volume producers that could exploit the manufacturing economies associated with large production runs. Despite its quality, the high price and low production volume of Dorris vehicles made it difficult for the firm to compete with high-volume producers as the automobile industry consolidated and integrated vertically. With prices ranging from $4,875 to $7,190 in 1922, the firm was unable to sell enough vehicles to remain viable.

Dorris production totaled just over 3,000 automobiles between 1906 and 1925, with peak production of 396 vehicles reached in 1920. Thereafter, production dwindled to 23 in the firm's final year of operation. After his automobile firm went under, Dorris remained in St. Louis and was a prominent citizen. The machinery manufacturing firm he subsequently founded continues in operation to the current day. In an interesting historical footnote, UM–St. Louis's Center for Emerging Technologies occupies the old Dorris factory facility.

The Gardner Motor Car Company was founded by Russell E. "Commodore" Gardner Sr. Gardner was one of St. Louis's prominent businessmen at the turn of the twentieth century as a result of the success of his carriage manufacturing firm. A 1903 article in the *St. Louis Post-Dispatch* calls "Commodore" Gardner "one of the luckiest, merriest men in St. Louis" who is "a hardheaded man of business" so rich that "you can just hear the money jingle when he goes by" ("Here They Are" 1903).

According to a 1924 Gardner Motor Car Company brochure, Russell Gardner Sr. started the Banner Buggy Business in 1875 which, after he moved to St. Louis in 1896 to start the Gardner Carriage Company, rapidly became "the largest buggy and specialty manufacturing plant in the world." Gardner grew increasingly wealthy as his buggy plant increased production twelvefold between 1896 and 1910. Nonetheless, he could see the writing on the wall, and Gardner converted the plant to the production of automobiles in 1914. He soon entered into an agreement with Chevrolet to build vehicles under license. The first Chevrolet was built in St. Louis in 1915, as the result of his efforts. *St. Louis Commerce* magazine notes: "In 1915, Russell E. Gardner Sr. under franchise of the Chevrolet Motor Co., turned his Banner Buggy Co. to the production of Louis Chevrolet's historic Model 490 passenger car, so called because it sold for $490" (Hannon 1966).

This plant was subsequently sold to Chevrolet (which had by then been acquired by the General Motors Corporation) in 1918. The Gardner Motor Car Company was formed in 1919, and Gardner bought the plant back from GM to manufacture his own vehicle. (Chevrolet, in turn, built the larger "north side plant" at the intersection of Union and Natural Bridge avenues, which would continue to operate until 1987.)

Gardner automobiles were produced from 1920 to 1931, with peak production of 9,000 units in 1922. As with the Dorris, Gardner vehicles were well regarded in their time but were relatively expensive, upscale vehicles. And, as with the Dorris Motor Car Company, the Gardner Motor Car Company was a victim of the Great Depression and was liquidated in 1931.

The last and perhaps most well known of St. Louis's Big Three is the Moon Motor Car Company. Like the Gardner Motor Car Company, Moon began in the buggy-making business and later switched to automobiles. The Moon Motor Car Company began as the Moon Brothers Buggy Company in 1882. It became the Joseph W. Moon Buggy Company in 1893, and in 1907 it was incorporated as the Moon Motor Car Company of St. Louis. While the firm continued to manufacture buggies and carriages for nine more years, Joseph Moon knew that the future lay in automobiles.

The first Moon vehicle was a five-passenger touring car produced in 1906, with a retail price of $3,000. Like George Dorris, Joseph Moon stressed quality in his vehicles. Where Dorris was an engineer and inventor, Moon was an "adapter." That is, Moon was more apt to selectively adopt the best features of its competitors, rather than develop them itself. As McConnell notes, "buying its engines and other components from suppliers, the St. Louis company built a solid, even luxurious, car and offered a large number of standard and special body styles. It studied other cars and freely borrowed new ideas that improved the appearance, comfort, or design of its own vehicles" (McConnell 1995, 222).

# That distinctively
## different motor car

SPEED • STAMINA

*THE* Gardner Eight-in-line is a distinctively different motor car because the spirit of the men who build it is one of distinctive difference. With them, true artistry and splendid craftsmanship are more greatly prized than high production records—and each increase in charm and distinction is hailed as a notable achievement.

THE GARDNER MOTOR CO.. INC., ST. LOUIS, U. S. A.

*GARDNER* now builds the Eight-in-line in 3 distinctive series—the 75, 85 and 95. Fifteen body styles are available—an endless array of interior and color combinations —at

*$1195 to $2495*

# G A R D N E R
## *Eight - in - Line*

Gardner Motor Car Company advertisement from period magazine, n.d.
Collection of the author.

Over its three decades of existence, the Moon Motor Car Company produced over 26,000 vehicles, many of which survive today and are highly prized by antique automobile collectors. At its peak the firm was selling vehicles through seven hundred dealers in fifty-five cities in the United States, as well as in forty-seven countries across the globe.

Unfortunately, the firm came to a sad and rather messy end. Unlike the Dorris Motor Car Company, which more or less quietly entered bankruptcy and vanished from the automotive scene, or the Gardner Motor Car Company, which liquidated voluntarily and paid its stockholders a handsome liquidating dividend, Moon collapsed as the result of a series of poor business decisions. The result of these decisions was that the firm engaged in a series of more and more desperate business maneuvers until, at the end, it was left to twist in the wind for over three decades while creditors picked over the corporate bones.

Joseph Moon died in 1919 and Stewart McDonald, formerly the firm's vice president and general manager, took over as president. The 1925 edition of *Who's Who in North St. Louis* describes McDonald as a "a brilliant young engineer" and a "dynamic man of the automotive industry, [who] has guided the company through the various ups and downs which have been visited upon the automobile industry during the past seven or eight years and this by reason of his far seeing business and executive ability and wise management" (North St. Louis Businessmens Association 1925).

Under McDonald's management, the firm initially prospered. However, he made a series of increasingly bad decisions: a failed attempt to sidestep the firm's distributor network and place cars directly with agencies ended disastrously after eighteen months, the production of the beautiful but severely flawed Diana automobile resulted in warranty claims that cost the firm tens of thousands of dollars and damaged its reputation, and a last-ditch attempt to manufacture the technologically advanced, but unproven front-drive Ruxton automobile placed the firm in dire financial straits.

In late 1929, McDonald obtained a loan from Wall Street financier Archie Andrews. Through a series of financial machinations, Andrews ultimately wrested control of the firm from McDonald and his management team. Between the lingering impacts of bad decisions and the onset of the Great Depression, the firm was doomed. A receiver was named on November 15, 1930, and automobile production ceased. The Moon story doesn't quite end there, however. The dissolution of the Moon Motor Car Company constitutes one of the longest bankruptcy proceedings on record—final payment to creditors over three decades later, in 1966.

# New Conditions Revolutionize
# Motor Car Design

RAFFIC conditions are changing fast—cars built almost yesterday are now out of date.

Thousands of miles of hard, fast roads tempt you to set your speedometer at 50 miles, hour after hour.

The old-type lubrication, three-bearing crankshaft, mechanical brakes, are not adequate for modern traffic strains. The four-bearing crankshaft of the new Moon eliminates all vibration. Moon's new pressure lubrication system stops undue wear at sustained high speed.

Balloon tires have come to stay—but with the old steering gear they "shimmy" and turn hard in traffic. With Moon's new patented steering gear, you can park downtown in a 14-foot space with one light twirl of the wheel.

Bold, progressive in design, the beauty of the new Sedan body tells its own story. You will find it the last word in "smartness" and comfort. See this new car and decide for yourself how well Moon has met the new style and engineering demands in a fine car at an economical price.

All Moon cars have six cylinders, improved four-wheel hydraulic brakes, with special patented steering gear, balloon tires and Duco finish.

MOON

OON MOTOR CAR COMPANY · ST. LOUIS, U. S. A

**Moon Motor Car Company advertisement from period magazine, n.d.
Collection of the author.**

## St. Louis's "Little Three": The St. Louis Motor Carriage Company, the St. Louis Car Company, and the St. Louis Automobile and Supply Company

The first auto factory in St. Louis was that of the St. Louis Motor Carriage Company, which built its first machine in 1898. Incorporated a year later with capital of $30,000, the firm's officers included Joseph, John, Calllie, Jesse, and H. E. French, and George Preston Dorris. An item in the April 19, 1899, issue of *The Horseless Age* notes the location of the firm's factory at 1211 N. Vandeventer and prints the illustration below as an example of "a light delivery wagon which has just left their shop" and "is to be put on the market in quantities." The firm's vehicles were advertised as "the kind you have been looking for. Compact, durable, easily managed."

**St. Louis Motor Carriage Company. National Automotive History Collection, Detroit Public Library.**

Before long, the firm was manufacturing relatively large numbers of the more advanced "St. Louis" automobile and distributing sophisticated catalogs. An early St. Louis Motor Carriage catalog proudly proclaims the logo that would become most associated with the firm: "Rigs That Run."

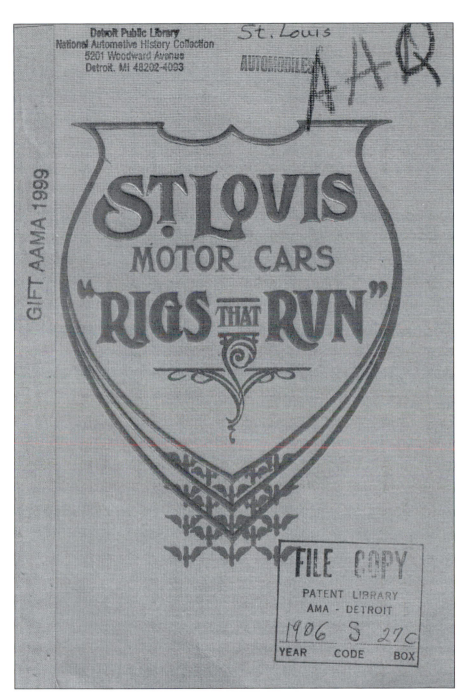

St. Louis
AUTOMOBILES
A A Q

## ST.LOUIS
### MOTOR CARS
### "RIGS THAT RUN"

St. Louis Motor Carriage Company product catalog.
National Automotive History Collection, Detroit Public Library.

The 1903 edition of the *St. Louis City Directory* also displays this logo prominently, along with an image of the firm's product.

STYLISH MILLINERY *Famous* BROADWAY AND MORGAN.

2124    AUC    GOULD'S 1903 DIRECTORY.    AUT

JOHN L. FRENCH, Pres.    G. P. DORRIS, Vice-Pres.    H. EDGAR FRENCH, Sec. & Treas.

## ST. LOUIS MOTOR CARRIAGE CO.

MANUFACTURERS OF THE

CELEBRATED "RIGS THAT RUN"

OFFICE, SALESROOMS AND FACTORY
1211=13=15=17=19 NORTH VANDEVENTER AVENUE.

**St. Louis Motor Carriage Company advertisement.**
**Gould's** *St. Louis City Directory*, **1903.**

With this catchy (if brief) motto, the St. Louis was a successful, if short-lived, make. And, as early firms went, it was a relatively prolific firm, producing approximately one thousand vehicles between 1899 and 1905. The firm was the source of a number of firsts. The St. Louis Motor Carriage Company was undoubtedly the first "real" automobile manufacturer in St. Louis. And, in personal correspondence, Andrew Lee Dyke states that John French, one of the firm's officers, made the first motor trip between St. Louis and Chicago in a 1900 model (Dyke n.d.).

In 1905, the firm's chief officer, John French, changed the name of the firm to the St. Louis Motor Car Company and moved it to Peoria, Illinois, with hopes for expansion. Unfortunately for the firm, its chief engineer, George Preston Dorris, chose to remain in St. Louis in order to begin his own automobile manufacturing company, and the company began to suffer business reverses almost immediately. In July 1907 it was announced that the firm would "continue operations under conditions decided upon by a committee of the creditors" under a plan by which "two-thirds of the proceeds derived from the sale of cars will be devoted to satisfying the claims of the creditors and one-third to the maintenance and operation of the plant. The factory will be taken charge of by a trustee named by the creditors and paid by them. It is stated that a new company will be formed to continue the business" (*The Horseless Age* 1907, 159).

The plan was unsuccessful—a bankruptcy receiver was appointed shortly thereafter, and the firm's assets were liquidated in November of that year.

The second member of St. Louis's "Little Three" is the St. Louis Car Company (SLCC). SLCC was not a small company by any measure; however, it was in the automobile business for only a short period. The firm is better known for its manufacture of streetcars and railway coaches; however, on November 1, 1906, the firm announced that it would soon be offering a licensed version of the French Mors automobile, which (not surprisingly) it would call the "American Mors." In the announcement, the firm noted that "results of the past few years have proven the superiority of the foreign type of car and for this reason we looked to Europe to furnish the design of car which we should build."

Though it was founded in 1887 as a builder of streetcars and trolleys, the St. Louis Car Company recognized the growing importance of personal transportation and elected to enter the automobile market. According to the *Standard Catalog of American Cars 1805–1942*, five-passenger touring cars, seven-passenger touring cars, and limousines were produced by the firm from 1906 to 1909 under license (Kimes and Clark 1996). The firm's management was nothing if not confident; a press release noted that the firm "enters the field under the most auspicious conditions, owing to the fact that they own and operate their own gray and malleable iron and brass foundries, and are, in consequence, able to obtain perfect castings for cylinders and other parts" (Lind 1978).

**AMERICAN MORS**

## AUTOMOBILES

### LIMOUSINES
### DEMI=LIMOUSINES
### TOURING CARS

14=18 H. P.    24=32 H. P.    40=52 H. P.

Perfect in Material, Workmanship
and Design

Made by

# St. Louis Car Company

ST. LOUIS, U. S. A.

Under license by Societe Anonyme a Electracite et d'Automobiles "Mors," Paris, France

Gould's *St. Louis City Directory*, 1907.

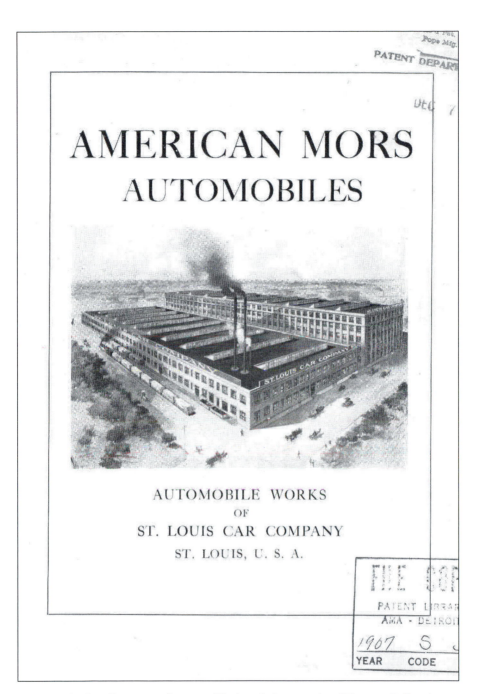

AMERICAN MORS
AUTOMOBILES

AUTOMOBILE WORKS
OF
ST. LOUIS CAR COMPANY
ST. LOUIS, U. S. A.

St. Louis Car Company factory. National Automotive History Collection,
Detroit Public Library.

The firm's success at producing the American Mors emboldened it to design and produce an automobile of its own. Thus, the St. Louis Car Company commenced production of a vehicle of its own design in 1909, the Standard Six. A year later, production of the Standard Six was moved to the firm's Indiana subsidiary. The shift in location was a bad idea, however; production of the vehicle ceased by the end of 1910.

The St. Louis Car Company was not yet out of the automobile business. From 1920 to 1922 the firm assembled 1,355 automobiles for the Skelton Motor Corporation. Unfortunately, this car proved no more long lived than its two predecessors, and the St. Louis Car Company focused on producing public transportation vehicles for the next five decades—it remained a successful streetcar, bus, and railroad car builder until the 1970s. Despite its somewhat spotty record, the firm succeeded in building and selling a vehicle of relatively sophisticated design under license, and had entered the ranks of St. Louis automobile producers (and subsequently left again) not once, but three times in a space of less than two decades.

One of the most important figures of this early period is Andrew Lee (A. L.) Dyke. Among his contributions to the early development of the automobile, Dyke created the country's first automobile supply company—the St. Louis Automobile and Supply Company. However, his firm did more than sell spark plugs—Dyke sold all of the components for one to manufacture his own vehicle. The most popular of these was Dyke's Number One Outfit, essentially the distant ancestor of today's "kit cars," which arrive at the enthusiast's home in numerous crates to be assembled at the buyer's leisure.

Dyke sold vehicles, parts, and supplies both to the walk-in trade and via mail-order catalog. The prominence of his firm is suggested by the size of his display at the 1904 World's Fair.

A close inspection of the image reveals that Dyke's firm not only supplied automobiles and components, but also motoring apparel—full-length dusters, goggles, caps, and so forth. Several sources suggest that his firm was so influential in the early years of motoring that a common term for the well-dressed motorist was that he or she was "all dyked up." Hochfelder and Helper (1996) write of Dyke that "foreseeing 'that the automobile supply business would become a distinct branch' of the industry, he threw over car building for parts jobbing in 1899." The resulting firm was Dyke's components firm, the St. Louis Automobile and Supply Company.

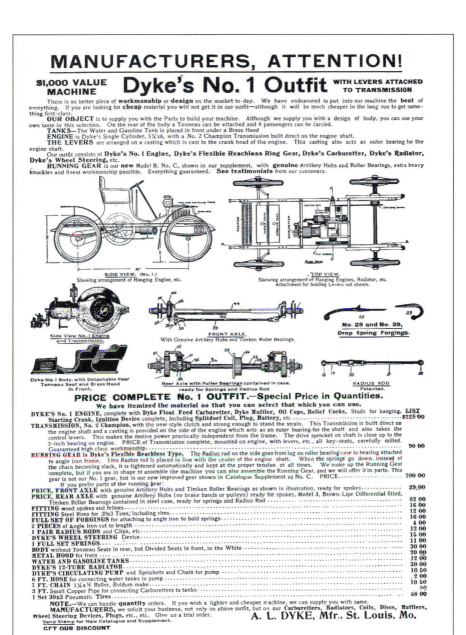

Dyke's Number One Outfit.
*The Horseless Age,* n.d. Collection of the author.

**A. L. Dyke Company display at the 1904 World's Fair.**
**National Automotive History Collection, Detroit Public Library.**

Interestingly, the catalog's first page states that the firm's object "is to supply the trade in general, also to individuals a **Complete Running Gear** with our **Improved Gasoline Engine** and **Transmission** device, mounted ready to receive the body. In this way parties who so desire can purchase our complete outfit, mount the body, paint and upholster and put it on the market at a reasonable figure and clear a good profit" (bold in original). The catalog's first page also contains the frequently repeated claim that Dyke's firm was "**the first company in any country** to attempt to carry a line of Automobile Supplies" (bold in original).[3]

---

[3] Whether or not this assertion is true may never be verified to complete satisfaction. Dyke began making this claim with his first catalog in 1900 and continued to do so in letters and papers written in the years shortly prior to his death nearly six decades later. In 1901 an industry publication announced the availability of the catalog in the following fashion: "The St. Louis Automobile & Supply Co., St. Louis, Mo., who claim to be the first company in the world to start an automobile supply business, have issued a catalogue of their various gears, transmissions, engines, and complete vehicles. They aim to handle nearly everything that enters into the construction of an automobile, and make a specialty of their complete running gear, improved gasoline engine and transmission, which they sell to experimenters or those who wish to build vehicles for themselves" (*The Horseless Age*, September 5, 1900).

# St. Louis Automobile and Supply Co.'s

### CATALOGUE OF

# Automobile Running Gears,

### Engines, Supplies, Etc.

### ALSO MANUFACTURERS OF

# Complete GASOLINE and ELECTRIC Vehicles

### OFFICE AND FACTORY:

# 23rd AND ST. CHARLES STREETS,

### ST. LOUIS, U. S. A.

**St. Louis Automobile and Supply Company 1900 catalog.
Collection of the author.**

**Vehicles of the St. Louis Automobile and Supply Company.
National Automotive History Collection, Detroit Public Library.**

Dyke's firm also produced a small number of vehicles. The above picture appears on the final page of the firm's 1900 catalog and is captioned: "The above illustration gives a view of a few vehicles which we make, with the exception of the rig in front; this rig we are agents for."

Dyke subsequently left the automobile supply business, but he remained an important figure in the growing industry by publishing automobile repair manuals—*Dyke's Automobile Encyclopedia*—annually until 1953, writing automotive-oriented columns for newspapers such as the *New York Times* and the *St. Louis Globe-Democrat*, and distributing "self-study" courses for would-be mechanics and enthusiasts.

The long-lasting influence of A. L. Dyke is suggested in the introduction to the 1954 edition of *Motor Service's New Automotive Encyclopedia*, which states: "Experience obtained in publishing and promoting the sale of Dyke's famous Automobile and Gasoline Engine Encyclopedia for the past thirty years (almost a million copies have been sold) has served as a guide to what should be included in this Encyclopedia and how it should be presented, in order to make it of most benefit to those who want a complete and authentic 'Bible' of automotive information" (Tobold and Purvis 1954).

Interestingly, Dyke and George Dorris remained friends for decades. The *Sunday Magazine* of the August 15, 1948, issue of the *St. Louis Post-Dispatch* provides extensive coverage of a road trip to Wisconsin made by the then-elderly pair in a 1902 St. Louis runabout to attend an antique auto show.

It is probably not a coincidence that all of the firms described above were out of business by the end of 1931. This is due in part to the fact that they were "assemblers" rather than "manufacturers" of automobiles. By and large, those American firms that survived until the end of the 1930s were vertically integrated manufacturers, not assemblers. It was, perhaps, St. Louis's misfortune to be home to assemblers rather than manufacturers. "The automobile manufacturers in Metropolitan St. Louis are scattered, one or two in each industrial section. Most of them are new companies, but a few are metamorphosed buggy and wagon companies, e.g., the Moon Motor Car Company from the Moon Buggy and Wagon Company. The twelve so-called automobile manufacturers in St. Louis are in reality assemblers of automobile parts, and they again illustrate the excellent advantages of St. Louis as a distributing point for assembled commodities" (Thomas 1927, 75).

Unfortunately, production techniques that drove costs down without reducing quality were rapidly transforming the industry and driving out the "assembly firms." The transition of industry production processes and the resulting shakeout among producers was rapid—the speed of the consolidation of the automobile industry is indicated in Epstein (1931), who notes that "the total number of companies engaged in the entire [United States] passenger car manufacturing business . . . ranged from eighty-nine in 1921 to thirty-eight in 1927." Further, he notes that in 1928 and 1929, several of the companies in the latter number closed due to failure or merger. By the end of the 1930s, St. Louis's independents were gone.

# Postwar Growth: St. Louis Becomes a Player—Again

> St. Louis, with its three big automotive plants turning out some 700,000 cars and trucks a year, may be only No. 2 in the country now. Someday, maybe, it will be No. 1.—*Robert E. Hannon, in* St. Louis Commerce Magazine, *November 1966*

In 1948, the *St. Louis Globe-Democrat* ran a series entitled "What Makes St. Louis Great?" In the article it was noted that the city had been "a great wagon-building center which supplied the whole southwest" and was second only to Detroit in the volume of automobile production. However, subsequent changes in the automobile industry caused St. Louis to relinquish its role. By the end of 2003, the state of Ohio had overtaken St. Louis as the second-largest automobile manufacturer in the United States, with 1.9 million vehicles produced. The story of how the city rose to that position, and subsequently fell from it, is another interesting part of the history of St. Louis and the automobile.

In 1955 the *St. Louis Post-Dispatch* proclaimed Missouri the second-ranking automobile producer in the nation because more than 523,000 vehicles were produced in Missouri in the previous year. A little over a decade later, *St. Louis Commerce Magazine* proudly proclaimed that "St. Louis is No. 2." St. Louis was home to manufacturing plants of each of "the big three," annual production exceeded 700,000 vehicles in 1965, and over 16,000 people were employed in automobile manufacturing. The article notes that "with 8,000 employees and an annual payroll of more than $68 million, the Chevrolet plant, with its companion Fisher Body Plant, stands next to McDonnell as the St. Louis area's largest employer" (Hannon 1966).

As noted previously, St. Louis's relationship with the major players extends almost to the beginning of the twentieth century. The first Ford plant was built here in 1914, and Chevrolets were built in St. Louis beginning in 1915.

The General Motors plant that was built at the intersection of Union and Natural Bridge in 1920 dominated automobile production in St. Louis for nearly seven decades. In addition to automobile assembly, General Motors' Fisher Body Division began building Chevrolet bodies at one end of the facility in 1922. By 1949, the facility employed 3,000 people, and sixteen years later, the number of employees there exceeded 8,000. Employment peaked at approximately 10,000 in the late 1970s. In addition to passenger cars and trucks, the plant was the sole manufacturer of the Corvette from 1953 until 1982. It is not difficult to see why Missouri reached "number two" in terms of postwar automobile production: From 1920 until its closing in 1987, the "north side plant" produced more than 13.3 million vehicles.

Adding to the area's automobile production is the Chrysler plant in Fenton. Second in local production in the mid-1960s, the plant employed more than 5,000 people and generated approximately $38 million in wages and benefits. Opened in 1959, the Chrysler plant produced 220,269 1966 models. In early 1964, the company announced plans to build a truck assembly plant nearby, which ultimately expanded production even further. Today, employment at the DaimlerChrysler facility far exceeds any of its peers at approximately 6,200 workers.

Not far behind in both its importance to the local economy and its contribution to production is the Ford plant in Hazelwood, where employment at one point reached 3,150 people with an annual payroll of over $25 million. Ford production began in St. Louis in 1914 at 4100 Forest Park Boulevard, and the Hazelwood plant was built in 1948. By 2000, the facility covered 3.1 million square feet, but employment had fallen to just over 2,600 people. In 2002 Ford Motor Company announced its intention to cease all production at the Hazelwood plant. Since then, city officials have continued to fight to keep the plant open. At this writing, the plant remains in operation, albeit at lower production levels. At the beginning of 2005, approximately 900 employees were laid off when second-shift production was discontinued. Employment in early 2006 stood at approximately 1,700, and the Ford Motor Company had been persuaded to continue operating the plant until at least 2007.

General Motors' Wentzville facility employs approximately 2,300 workers. Built to replace the aging and increasingly inefficient north side plant, the GM Wentzville facility has been modestly successful, both in terms of labor relations and production efficiency. A 2004 *Post-Dispatch* article notes that the Wentzville plant "was the most productive full-size-van facility in North America" in 2003, and that "the union-management relationship has been a key factor" according to the GM group vice president for manufacturing and labor relations (Cancelada 2004).

# St. Louis Auto Manufacturing on the Decline—Again

Today, St. Louis is no longer second to Detroit in domestic automobile manufacturing, due in no small part to the transfer of production offshore, as well as to the declining market share of the major domestic automakers. Over the last three decades, the market share of GM, Ford, and Chrysler has fallen from over 50 percent to approximately 25 percent, and dozens of assembly plants have closed or been downsized in order to reduce capacity to meet declining demand. In late 2005, plans were announced by GM head Rick Wagoner to lay off another 25,000 employees and further reduce production capacity. Foreign automakers, on the other hand, have opened twenty-three North American manufacturing and assembly plants in the last ten years, primarily in the southeastern United States.

St. Louis's postwar pre-eminence in automobile manufacturing was attributable in large part to the General Motors north side plant, which operated from February 1920 through August 1987. At its peak in the late 1970s, the plant employed nearly 10,000 people, making it second only to Anheuser-Busch as the largest employer in the city. By the time of its closing, this number had dwindled to just over 2,200 workers.

The closing of the north side plant was seen by many as the end of an era. The closing was not entirely unexpected. Non-air-conditioned, inefficient, and out of compliance with environmental regulations, the plant was described in a *Post-Dispatch* article as "a filthy hotbox" that was "doomed to obsolescence" (Wagman 1987). As if that weren't enough, the plant had been well known for an exceptional amount of labor-management hostility since at least the 1970s, when the strife erupted in a number of suspicious fires and sabotage. By 1978, things had become so bad that GM's director of labor relations wrote that "this sabotage has been reviewed by the highest officers of the General Motors Corp. and they are alarmed. There is deep concern over the future of the St. Louis plant" (Wagman 1987).

Originally GM's plan was to close the north side plant and transfer the employees to its shiny new facility in Wentzville. Unfortunately, the old plant remained open longer than originally planned, and the Wentzville facility commenced operation before the north side plant closed. The eventual transfer of St. Louis employees to Wentzville was accompanied by loss of seniority for some employees, who were either "bumped" out of current jobs or laid off. Not surprisingly, this resulted in labor strife, hard feelings, and production problems.

Newspaper articles of the period indicated that the north side plant might be acquired by a foreign manufacturer or razed to create an industrial park or a horse-racing track. Today, the area is home to the Union Seventy Center Business Park, a conglomeration of businesses able to effectively utilize the space.

# The Domestic Automobile Industry's Secular Decline

While still important to the economy of Missouri and the St. Louis region, automobile manufacturing no longer plays the central role it once did. For three decades the relative economic impact of the Big Three has been declining, as a result of falling domestic production and, therefore, employment, and because of shifts in emphasis to large and growing automobile markets elsewhere, such as those in China and India. North American employment by the Big Three domestic automakers has fallen by slightly over 25 percent since 2000—from 520,152 workers to 389,758. Over the same period, North American production by foreign "transplant" firms—Honda, Nissan, and Toyota, among others—has increased by nearly 31 percent, mostly in states outside of Missouri (Kachadourian 2005). The leader among these firms is Toyota, which employs over 37,000 workers in thirteen manufacturing plants in North America. Toyota's sales in the United States outpaced its sales in Japan for the first time in 2000, and the firm now produces more vehicles in America than any other foreign manufacturer. The firm's 2004 profit exceeded that of the General Motors, Ford, and Chrysler combined. Global Insight, Inc., predicts that Toyota's annual output will equal that of General Motors by 2010.

As this is written, the next few years are likely to be difficult for at least two of the Big Three. General Motors has replaced its head of North American operations as a result of poor performance, and the bonds of General Motors and Ford have been downgraded to "junk" status. Higher borrowing costs are likely to result, and the two firms face rapidly increasing pension and health-care costs at a time when many of the new models that were expected to excite customers and ignite sales have failed to catch on. International markets have become highly competitive, and other producers seem better positioned to gain market share. And if all this weren't enough, domestic producers, which have already lost substantial market share to Japanese manufacturers, now face increased competition from up-and-coming Korean and Chinese firms. It is undoubtedly too soon to pronounce the domestic automobile industry dead, but it is unlikely that it will soon return to the dominant global position it commanded for most of the twentieth century.

What will St. Louis's role be in the automobile industry going forward? Although early 2006 brought an announcement that the long-standing Ford plant in Hazelwood would cease operations in a few years, Ford had previously announced a shift in production from a plant closed in Ohio to one in Claycomo, Missouri. The auto and truck manufacturing plants in Wentzville continue strong production. Also, St. Louis retains many of those factors that make it an ideal manufacturing location—rivers, railroads, and a large labor pool. Perhaps the continued U.S. growth of foreign automakers will bring new production facilities to the St. Louis region, as it has elsewhere. Perhaps state officials can convince the heads of the domestic automakers that Missouri is indeed "business friendly" and that they should return production to St. Louis. History indicates that it's not a bad bet.

## Acknowledgments

Library personnel at the University of Missouri–St. Louis, particularly Ms. Mary Zettwoch and Mr. Jim Rhoads, have been tremendously helpful in this effort. Additionally, Mark Patterson, curator of the National Automotive History Collection of the Detroit Public Library, was of great help. Finally, a debt of gratitude is owed to my assistant, Ms. Jamillah Boyd, for her help in keeping my "official" obligations at bay while this manuscript was being prepared.

### References

Borth, Christy. "Wheels for a Waiting World: The Story of General Motors." *Ward's Quarterly* (Spring 1966): 89–108.

Burgess, Tad. *Cars of the Early Twenties*. Philadelphia: Chilton Book Company, 1968.

Cancelada, Gregory. "Wentzville Plant Earns Distinction as Most Productive." *St. Louis Post-Dispatch*, June 11, 2004.

*Collier's Yearbook*. New York: P.F. Collier & Son Corporation, 1949.

Dyke, Andrew Lee. Papers. Detroit Public Library, Michigan.

Epstein, Ralph C. "Profits and the Size of the Firm in the Automobile Industry, 1919–1927." *The American Economic Review 21*, no. 4 (December 1931): 636–647.

Hannon, Robert E. "St. Louis Is No. 2." *St. Louis Commerce Magazine*, November 1966, 8–11.

"Here They Are—The Luckiest, Wisest and Merriest Men in St. Louis." *St. Louis Post-Dispatch*, June 7, 1903.

Hochfelder, David, and Susan Helper. "Suppliers and Product Development in the Early American Automobile Industry." *Business and Economic History 25*, no. 2 (1996): 39–51.

*Horseless Age, The*, April 19, 1899.

*Horseless Age, The*, September 5, 1900.

Kachadourian, Gail. "Auto Jobs: A Big Tilt Away from the Big Three." *Automotive News*, April 25, 2005.

Kimes, Beverly Rae, and Henry Austin Clark Jr. *Standard Catalog of American Cars 1805–1942*. 3rd ed. Iola, WI: Krause Publications, 1996.

Kollins, Michael J. *Pioneers of the U.S. Automobile Industry.* Vol. 2, *The Small Independents.* Warrendale, PA: Society of Automotive Engineers, 2002.

Langlois, Richard, and Paul L. Robertson. "Explaining Vertical Integration: Lessons from the American Automobile Industry." *The Journal of Economic History* 49, no. 2 (1989): 361–375.

Lind, Alan R. *From Horsecars to Streamliners: An Illustrated History of the St. Louis Car Company.* Park Forest, IL: Transport History Press, 1978.

McConnell, Curt. *Great Cars of the Great Plains.* Lincoln: University of Nebraska Press, 1995.

Nicholson, T. R. *Passenger Cars, 1863–1904.* New York: Macmillan Company, 1970.

Nicklaus, David. "St. Louis Auto Industry Still Could Be Headed for a Crash." *St. Louis Post-Dispatch*, January 18, 2004.

North St. Louis Businessmens Association. *Who's Who in North St. Louis.* St. Louis: [A. S. Werremeyer], 1925.

"Of Commercial Interest." *Horseless Age*, June 27, 1900, p. 25.

"Of Commercial Interest." *Horseless Age,* July 31, 1907, p. 159.

Primm, James Neal. *A Foregone Conclusion: The Founding of the Federal Reserve Bank of St. Louis.* St. Louis: Federal Reserve Bank of St. Louis, 1989.

———. *Lion of the Valley: St. Louis, Missouri.* Boulder, CO: Pruett Publishing Company, 1990.

Rae, John B. *American Automobile Manufacturers: The First Forty Years.* Philadelphia: Chilton Company, 1959.

St. Louis Society of Automobile Pioneers. *Four Wheels, No Brakes!* St. Louis: Von Hoffman Press, 1930.

Thomas, Lewis F. *The Localization of Business Activities in Metropolitan St. Louis.* St. Louis: Washington University Studies—New Series, 1927.

Thomas, Robert Paul. *An Analysis of the Pattern of Growth of the Automobile Industry, 1895–1929.* New York: Arno Press, 1977.

Tobold, William K., and Jud Purvis. *Motor Service's New Automotive Encyclopedia.* Chicago: The Goodheart-Willcox Co., 1954.

Wagman, Paul. "Labor Relations Fall Short of GM Hopes." *St. Louis Post-Dispatch*, February 22, 1987, pp. A1, A10–A11.

# Chapter 3

# Technology Transfer and the Modern University

**Nasser Arshadi, Harvey A. Harris, and Thomas F. George**

In the past two decades, universities across the United States have focused on the importance of commercializing the discoveries emerging from their laboratories. Most have taken significant steps toward putting the necessary infrastructure in place to transfer important discoveries to market, establishing offices of technology transfer and various proof-of-concept funds.

Such infrastructure is critical because while scientists are the intellectual backbone of technology transfer, they are not always equipped with the expertise necessary to commercialize their discoveries. The technology transfer offices that have mushroomed on university campuses in recent years are responsible for obtaining patents, negotiating license agreements, and helping guide faculty through the intricate process of establishing start-up companies. Creating a start-up company requires a variety of tasks to be performed, including writing a business plan; recruiting financial backers, key employees, and board members; conducting market research; performing clinical trials; and launching products. If the company is initially successful, additional funding must be raised through venture capital financing and the stock market, which requires complex expertise in securities regulations and valuation of technologies, stocks, and stock options.

Research has shown that only 12 percent of a product's value is due to the invention, and the remainder is created in the process of technology transfer and commercialization, especially by discovering applications unforeseen by the original researchers (Sample 2001). An effective technology transfer strategy will lead to a significant increase in the number of discoveries disclosed, patents executed, licenses issued, and prosperous start-up companies established. These resulting businesses will create employment and contribute to the expansion of the economy. It is no surprise that 80 percent of new jobs are created by small businesses.

Although university technology transfer efforts have led to the commercialization of an impressive array of technologies and products (i.e., DNA testing, gene sequencing, Gatorade™), the current rate of technology transfer measured by the number of patents issued to academic institutions is relatively small. This is a surprise, considering the magnitude of R&D (research and development) expenditures at the universities.

This chapter presents a rigorous assessment of technology transfer efforts in academic institutions with the goal of identifying critical factors for a successful strategy. Equally important is to identify obstacles facing these institutions, the least of which is a general lack of business culture and knowledge of the marketplace.

The remainder of this chapter will address the following points and questions. A theoretical discussion illuminates the importance of technology transfer in linking R&D expenditures to increased productivity through innovation. A close examination of national and regional data shows the extent of university engagement in technology transfer and hence in economic development. An exploration of factors determining a successful strategy in technology transfer and commercialization is followed by a closer look at the experience in the St. Louis region. The region has a history of tremendous economic expansion only to be followed by decades of decline. What can a concerted effort in technology transfer and commercialization accomplish in such an environment? How can universities, research centers, and other sources of knowledge creation partner with the political and economic leadership to enhance the reach of technology transfer in order to make a lasting impact on the well-being of the region's citizens?

# Theoretical Foundation

Technology transfer is the process of taking an invention from its inception in a laboratory to a commercialized product. In the traditional view of universities, overt commercialization was antithetic to the pure goal of scientific inquiry. The modern view, however, assigns a critical role to research universities in technology transfer and commercialization. This view has been further bolstered by legislative rulings on the disposition of intellectual property rights (Weber and Duderstadt 2004; Bremer 2003).

At the core of technology transfer lies innovation, which is best quantified by the number of patents issued in a given year. A patent is a property right granted by the U.S. government to an inventor "to exclude others from making, using, offering for sale, or selling the invention throughout the United States or importing the invention into the United States" (United States Patent and Trademark Office [USPTO] 2005). The first U.S. patent was issued in 1790, and in the next two hundred years, 100,000 more patents were issued. During this period, the U.S. government held most of the patents obtained through research it had funded. From the 28,000 patents accumulated, the U.S. government had licensed only 4 percent. In 1980, Congress passed the Bayh-Dole Act allowing universities and other not-for-profit entities with government-sponsored research grants to retain the titles to their inventions. Consequently, the number of patents issued each year tripled from 1980 to 2003 when the USPTO issued a staggering 187,000 patents, of which 53 percent were issued to residents of the United States (Figure 1). During the same period, the share of university-owned patents increased from less than 1 percent to 3.5 percent of total patents in the United States (Figure 2 represents the last decade of this period). Table 1 presents the number of patents issued to the U.S. residents of each state in 2003 (Winner 1999; Allan 2001; Gates and Rader 2001).

## Figure 1. U.S. Patent Statistics, 1980–2003

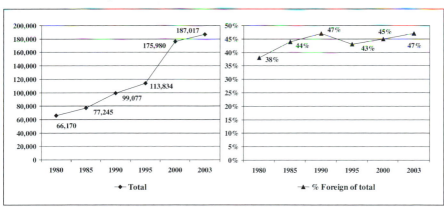

Source: U.S. Patent and Trademark Office.

## Figure 2. University Patents as % of Total U.S.-Owned Patents

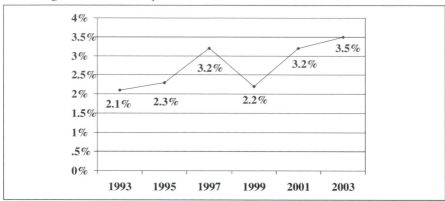

Source: Association of University Technology Managers.

## Table 1. Patents Issued to Residents of the United States: FY 2003

| State/Territory | No. for 2003 | State/Territory | No. for 2003 | State/Territory | No. for 2003 |
|---|---|---|---|---|---|
| Total | 99,898 | Minnesota | 3,243 | West Virginia | 148 |
| | | Tennessee | 1,009 | Hawaii | 78 |
| Kentucky | 483 | Colorado | 2,345 | New Jersey | 4,068 |
| Oklahoma | 566 | Mississippi | 186 | Wisconsin | 2,138 |
| Louisiana | 451 | Texas | 6,509 | Idaho | 1,883 |
| Oregon | 1,880 | Connecticut | 1,940 | New Mexico | 403 |
| Alabama | 458 | Missouri | 937 | Wyoming | 79 |
| Maine | 159 | Utah | 753 | Illinois | 3,979 |
| Pennsylvania | 3,592 | Delaware | 376 | New York | 6,973 |
| Alaska | 41 | Montana | 118 | Puerto Rico | 29 |
| Maryland | 1,623 | Vermont | 465 | Indiana | 1,720 |
| Rhode Island | 327 | District of Columbia | 57 | North Carolina | 2,199 |
| Arizona | 1,743 | Nebraska | 233 | U.S. Pacific Islands [2] | - |
| Massachusetts | 4,199 | Virginia | 1,250 | Iowa | 675 |
| South Carolina | 687 | Florida | 3,113 | North Dakota | 74 |
| Arkansas | 191 | Nevada | 424 | United States [3] | 1 |
| Michigan | 4,266 | Washington | 2,570 | Kansas | 510 |
| South Dakota | 89 | Georgia | 1,611 | Ohio | 3,972 |
| California | 22,351 | New Hampshire | 721 | Virgin Islands | 3 |

Source: United States Patent and Trademark Office.
Notes:
1. Data include utility, plant, design, and reissue patents.
2. Represents residents of American Samoa, Guam, and miscellaneous U.S. Pacific Islands.
3. No state indicated in database.

Hidden Assets

This is a clear shift in philosophy for research universities where creation and commercialization of knowledge coexist in relative harmony. In fact, a large number of public research universities have added economic development to their core mission, and technology transfer and commercialization are effective means to that goal (Jamison and Jansen 2000; Pressman 2002).

To fully appreciate the impact of technology transfer and commercialization on economic development, consider the following disposition of production function in economics:

$$Q = f(K, L, R)$$
$$Q = \alpha \, K\beta \, L\gamma \, R\lambda$$

$Q$ = *quantity of output*
$\alpha$ = *Intercept*
$K$ = *capital input*
$\beta$ = *rate of productivity of capital*
$L$ = *labor input*
$\gamma$ = *rate of productivity of labor*
$R$ = *R & D*
$\lambda$ = *rate of tech transfer*

The quantity of output, which reflects productivity, is a function of investments in capital, labor, and R&D. A detailed expression of this function includes the relative importance of sources of input—capital, labor, and R&D—in the final output. For example, investment in capital does not automatically lead to higher output without a mechanism in place to ensure it is effectively utilized. Similarly, investment in R&D does not necessarily lead to higher output; it does so only if there is an effective technology transfer strategy in place. In short, the exposition above provides us with the following observations:

investment in R&D is a necessary but not a sufficient condition for economic growth;

increase in R&D expenditures must be accompanied by effective means to increase the elasticity of the R&D output; and

productivity gains result only from the natural diffusion of innovation to the marketplace (i.e., technology transfer).

# A Closer Look at R&D Expenditures and the Rate of Technology Transfer

In fiscal year (FY) 2003, universities and colleges across the United States reported a total of $40.1 billion in research expenditures (Table 2). This is 10.2 percent more than the expenditures in FY 2002 and double the amount in FY 1993. The impressive expansion in research expenditures is primarily due to increases in funding through federal agencies. The federal share of the total expenditures reached almost 62 percent, and the remaining 38 percent included support from universities and colleges (19 percent), direct contributions from state and local government (6.6 percent), and industry (5.4 percent).

Although research expenditures in all fields affect innovation, those in science and engineering have the most direct impact. The medical sciences ($12.8 billion) and biological sciences ($7.4 billion) combined accounted for half of the total amount of research expenditures in FY 2003. In fact, 54 percent of all federal research dollars were spent in these fields (Table 3). The largest amount of research funding was provided by the Department of Health and Human Services (HHS), primarily through its National Institutes of Health (NIH). Support for engineering was provided by the Department of Defense (DOD) and the National Science

**Table 3. R&D Expenditures at Universities and Colleges, by Source of Funds and Science and Engineering Field: FY 2003 (millions of current dollars)**

| Source and Field | All R&D Expenditures | Federal R&D Expenditures | DOD | DOE |
|---|---|---|---|---|
| All R&D expenditures | 40,077 | 24,734 | 2,008 | 822 |
| Agricultural sciences | 2,555 | 762 | 10 | 15 |
| Biological sciences | 7,392 | 5,017 | 97 | 64 |
| Computer sciences | 1,304 | 936 | 297 | 29 |
| Environmental sciences | 2,188 | 1,440 | 91 | 72 |
| Mathematical sciences | 429 | 295 | 31 | 6 |
| Medical sciences | 12,787 | 8,249 | 156 | 37 |
| Physical sciences | 3,273 | 2,353 | 245 | 303 |
| Psychology | 769 | 553 | 22 | 2 |
| Social sciences | 1,661 | 667 | 18 | 10 |
| Engineering | 5,999 | 3,608 | 989 | 266 |

Source: National Science Foundation/Division of Science Resources Statistics, Survey of Research and Development Expenditures at Universities and Colleges, FY 2003.

Note: Because of rounding, detail by agency may not add to total. Not all fields are reported in this table.

Foundation (NSF). Other fields of inquiry including physical, environmental, and computer sciences also received funding from the NSF. Support for fields other than science and engineering was relatively small, with a total of $1.3 billion in FY 2003 (Table 4).

**Table 2. R&D Expenditures at Universities and Colleges: FY 1998–2003**
**(millions of current dollars)**

| Source and Character of Work | 1998 | 1999 | 2000 | 2001 | 2002 | 2003 |
|---|---|---|---|---|---|---|
| All expenditures | 25,855 | 27,530 | 30,067 | 32,797 | 36,370 | 40,077 |
| **Source of Funds** | | | | | | |
| Federal government | 15,150 | 16,101 | 17,535 | 19,223 | 21,860 | 24,734 |
| State and local governments | 1,944 | 2,021 | 2,200 | 2,321 | 2,506 | 2,653 |
| Industry | 1,888 | 2,033 | 2,156 | 2,220 | 2,187 | 2,162 |
| Institutional funds | 5,002 | 5,380 | 5,923 | 6,607 | 7,128 | 7,683 |
| All other sources | 1,870 | 1,994 | 2,254 | 2,426 | 2,689 | 2,845 |
| **Character of Work** | | | | | | |
| Basic research | 19,040 | 20,366 | 22,442 | 24,385 | 27,280 | 29,981 |
| Applied R&D | 6,815 | 7,163 | 7,625 | 8,412 | 9,090 | 10,097 |

Source: National Science Foundation/Division of Science Resources Statistics, Survey of Research and Development Expenditures at Universities and Colleges, FY 2003.
Note: Because of rounding, detail may not add to total.

| HHS | NASA | NSF | USDA | Other Agencies | Unspecified Agencies |
|---|---|---|---|---|---|
| 10,930 | 938 | 2,404 | 634 | 2,723 | 4,275 |
| 30 | 15 | 54 | 369 | 146 | 123 |
| 3,428 | 41 | 295 | 135 | 339 | 618 |
| 21 | 28 | 291 | 2 | 101 | 167 |
| 22 | 182 | 344 | 25 | 392 | 312 |
| 34 | 5 | 124 | 2 | 25 | 68 |
| 5,846 | 42 | 26 | 21 | 592 | 1,530 |
| 304 | 280 | 559 | 6 | 189 | 467 |
| 364 | 9 | 37 | 0 | 45 | 72 |
| 229 | 12 | 82 | 31 | 194 | 89 |
| 158 | 308 | 526 | 27 | 551 | 782 |

**Table 4. R&D Expenditures in Non-Science and Engineering Fields at Universities and Colleges: FY 2003 (millions of current dollars)**

| | |
|---|---:|
| All non-S&E R&D expenditures | 1,371 |
| Business and management | 165 |
| Communications, journalism, and library science | 55 |
| Education | 597 |
| Humanities | 135 |
| Law | 41 |
| Social work | 56 |
| Visual and performing arts | 39 |
| Other non-S&E fields | 241 |

Source: National Science Foundation/Division of Science Resources Statistics, Survey of Research and Development Expenditures at Universities and Colleges, FY 2003.
Note: Because of rounding, detail may not add to total.

There are different ways of gauging the intensity rate of technology transfer activities. One such measure is the number of patents issued per dollars of research expenditures. According to a FY 2003 survey by the Association of University Technology Managers (AUTM), universities incurred more than $10 million in research expenditures for each patent received. From an almost 100,000 patents issued to U.S. citizens in FY 2003, universities' share was only 3,450, a mere 3.5 percent.

Considering that the total amount of research expenditures, including non-university research activities, amounted to $300 billion in FY 2003, the overall technology transfer intensity rate was 1 patent per $3 million in research expenditures. In Missouri, most recent data shows total annual research expenditures of $2.5 billion supporting 937 patents issued to the residents of the state, or 1 patent per $2.66 million. The intensity rate of university technology transfer with 1 patent per $10 million compares unfavorably with national data. Another reading of this result suggests that despite major inroads for university technology transfer in recent years, 70 percent of total research expenditures produce no patentable discovery. On the licensing front, the gross income received by all U.S. universities surpassed $1 billion in FY 2003 (Table 5).

Although universities license many of their inventions to existing companies, they develop other discoveries through start-up companies. The decision to establish a start-up company around an invention instead of simply licensing it is related to one or both of the following factors: (1) established companies do not want new technologies that could potentially

**Table 5. AUTM Licensing Survey:**
**Summary of Fiscal Year (FY 2003) Totals, All Respondents**

| | |
|---|---:|
| Research expenditures: industrial sources | $2,537,020,737 |
| Research expenditures: federal govt. sources | $23,062,609,472 |
| Total sponsored research expenditures | $34,826,920,266 |
| Licenses/options executed | 3,855 |
| Start-up companies formed | 348 |
| Gross license income received | $1,033,609,726 |
| Legal fees expended | $176,278,483 |
| Legal fees reimbursed | $74,971,227 |
| Licenses/options yielding license income | 8,976 |
| Invention disclosures received | 13,718 |
| Total U.S. patent applications filed | 11,755 |
| New U.S. patent applications filed | 7,203 |
| U.S. patents issued | 3,450 |

Source: AUTM Licensing Survey FY 2003 Summary.

make their existing technologies obsolete; (2) the inventions are high-risk/high-return projects where their potential can be explored only through establishing start-up companies. In any case, universities have embarked on establishing a large number of start-up companies since 1980, totaling 4,117 with 2,279 companies still operating as of the end of FY 2003 (Table 6). Seventy-nine percent of these companies are located in the state of the academic institution.

**Table 6. Start-ups Formed by U.S. Respondents, 1980–2003**

| | Fiscal Year | | | | | | | | | | | |
|---|---|---|---|---|---|---|---|---|---|---|---|---|
| | 1980–1993 | 1994 | 1995 | 1996 | 1997 | 1998 | 1999 | 2000 | 2001 | 2002 | 2003 | 1980–2003 |
| Number of institutions responding | 136 | 145 | 157 | 156 | 155 | 157 | 168 | 167 | 167 | 183 | 190 | |
| Number of institutions reporting one or more | 128 | 75 | 84 | 77 | 86 | 98 | 98 | 116 | 116 | 118 | 120 | |
| Start-up companies formed | 1,013 | 212 | 192 | 202 | 275 | 306 | 294 | 424 | 424 | 401 | 374 | **4,117** |

Source: AUTM Licensing Survey FY 2003 Summary.

In their early years, start-up companies rarely have positive cash flows and, therefore, are unable to pay up-front fees for licensing rights they seek from universities. In such cases, universities often take equity positions in exchange for exclusive licensing rights. In FY 2003, universities received an equity interest in 67 percent of their start-up companies (Table 7).

**Table 7. Licenses and Start-Ups with Equity by U.S. Respondents, 1995–2003**

|  | 1995 | 1996 | 1997 | 1998 | 1999 | 2000 | 2001 | 2002 | 2003 |
|---|---|---|---|---|---|---|---|---|---|
| Number of institutions reporting one or more | 60 | 61 | 67 | 69 | 68 | 78 | 90 | 108 | 192 |
| Licenses with equity | 114 | 142 | 216 | 229 | 199 | 320 | 351 | 411 | 351 |
| Number of institutions reporting one or more | NA | NA | NA | NA | NA | 71 | 88 | 99 | 120 |
| Start-ups with equity | NA | NA | NA | NA | NA | 215 | 305 | 285 | 252 |

Source: AUTM Licensing Survey FY 2003 Summary.
Note: NA: Not available.

# Determinants of an Effective Technology Transfer Strategy

With the passage of the Bayh-Dole Act in 1980, the U.S. regulatory environment became substantially more hospitable toward technology transfer. Equally accommodating has been the financial market. The flow of capital from venture capital firms and the stock market gave rise to significant expansion in technology transfer in the late 1990s, and despite considerable slowdown in recent years, there still exists a healthy and vibrant technology transfer environment.

In early years, as a growing number of universities engaged in technology transfer, there were steady increases in the number of start-up companies being formed. This pattern continued until the late 1990s, when a major correction in the stock market strained the funding flow into new companies. Prior to 1999, finding financial backing for start-ups was relatively easy because venture capital firms could divest themselves when start-ups issued stocks publicly, which happened in exceedingly shorter periods of time. This changed by 2001 when the demand for start-up stocks declined significantly. At the peak of demand for new company stocks in 1999, there were 486 companies that issued stocks for the first time through initial public offering (IPO). The figure had dropped to 83 by 2001. During this period, IPO returns dropped from their market-adjusted rate of return of 111 percent in 1999 to 2 percent in 2001. The same pattern was seen for venture capital funding, which went from an all-time high of $105 billion in 2000 to $19 billion in 2003. There has been an uptick recently in the amount of venture capital investment with $21 billion in 2004. Tables 8 and 9 demonstrate the pattern. The decline in available funding also affected the number of companies formed around university inventions. Today, the number of start-ups being formed from university inventions is actually lower than in 2000.

### Table 8. 2003 Annual IPO Review

| IPO Summary Stats | | | | | | |
|---|---|---|---|---|---|---|
| | 1998 | 1999 | 2000 | 2001 | 2002 | 2003 |
| Number of deals | 247 | 486 | 406 | 83 | 70 | 68 |
| Total proceeds (billions) | $45 | $93 | $97 | $41 | $24 | $15 |
| Average deal size (millions) | $181 | $191 | $240 | $491 | $338 | $224 |
| **IPO Returns** | | | | | | |
| | | 1999 | 2000 | 2001 | 2002 | 2003 |
| Total return | | 276% | -18% | 16% | 3% | 28% |
| Aftermarket return | | 111% | -38% | 2% | -5% | 14% |

Source: IPOhome 2003 Annual Review.

### Table 9. U.S. Venture Capital Investment by Year—MoneyTree

| Year | Number of Deals | Avg. per Deal (USD Millions) | Investment ($M) |
|---|---|---|---|
| 1990 | 1,433 | 1.93 | 2,767.1 |
| 1991 | 1,231 | 1.82 | 2,241.7 |
| 1992 | 1,345 | 2.61 | 3,511.1 |
| 1993 | 1,161 | 3.19 | 3,708.1 |
| 1994 | 1,197 | 3.44 | 4,120.6 |
| 1995 | 1,776 | 4.42 | 7,853.5 |
| 1996 | 2,464 | 4.46 | 10,992.9 |
| 1997 | 3,084 | 4.75 | 14,646.9 |
| 1998 | 3,557 | 5.88 | 20,899.8 |
| 1999 | 5,403 | 9.92 | 53,579.6 |
| 2000 | 7,832 | 13.38 | 104,827.4 |
| 2001 | 4,451 | 9.17 | 40,798.4 |
| 2002 | 3,042 | 7.09 | 21,579.3 |
| 2003 | 2,825 | 6.69 | 18,911.0 |
| 2004 | 2,873 | 7.31 | 21,004.4 |

Source: PricewaterhouseCoopers/Thomson Venture Economics / National Venture Capital Association MoneyTree™ Survey—updated March 28, 2005.

In addition to factors described on the previous page, there is a significant need for a steady supply of professional managers to staff the offices of technology transfer and to manage the operation of start-up companies. Unlike the favorable regulatory and financial conditions described above, a dearth of trained managers remains as a major obstacle to a vibrant technology transfer environment.

The skill sets required to run an effective technology transfer office or to manage a start-up company are quite different from those required to manage an established company. Effective technology transfer and start-up managers must have sufficient expertise to conduct the following tasks (Arshadi and Karels 1997):

> make sound decisions as to whether a technology constitutes an innovation with commercial potential and whether an intellectual property (IP) protection needs to be sought;

> value technology and IP rights using established financial methods;

> decide whether a technology should be licensed or used to establish a start-up company;

> negotiate an optimum licensing fee structure instead of using an industry rule of thumb (i.e., 4 percent);

> negotiate with suppliers of capital with sufficient understanding of financial intricacies (i.e., dealings with angel and venture capital firms early on and investment banking firms in the process of going public);

> recruit, train, and retain human capital and establish contracts to mitigate conflict of interests;

> conduct market research;

> perform clinical trials;

> seek regulatory approval; and

> launch products.

Training for these skills is not fully integrated in the established business or legal curricula. For example, a typical MBA program is often designed to address the problems faced by a large publicly traded company rather than a start-up. Similarly, there is no known law school that currently trains students to handle these functions. Universities that offer combined

MBA/law programs still focus primarily on large publicly traded companies. An ideal program will train students in the following fields:

*Module One:*

> writing business plans
>
> formulating growth strategies
>
> managing new fast-growing firms
>
> competing in specific industries

*Module Two:*

> project, technology, and company valuation models
>
> risk and return
>
> capital budgeting under uncertainty
>
> stock and stock options pricing
>
> governance, contracting, and incentive issues
>
> venture capital and private equity

*Module Three:*

> overview of all intellectual property categories
>
> how intellectual property law works
>
> intellectual property strategy: identifying, protecting, and managing
>
> valuation models
>
> valuation: intellectual property rights
>
> valuation: venture capital point of view
>
> valuation: accounting and banking point of view

*Module Four:*

> trade secret law
>
> commercial and investment banking for technology businesses
>
> opportunities for tax incentives and credits
>
> state and local tax issues
>
> product development tools and trends
>
> public relations, marketing, and communications

*Module Five:*

> patent law
>
> how to protect intellectual property
>
> SBIR/STTR and other federal grants
>
> strategic partnerships
>
> sponsored research
>
> clinical trials and regulatory approval
>
> licensing in and out
>
> understanding equity

*Module Six:*

> stock and stock option valuation models
>
> venture capital presentations
>
> negotiating with venture capital firms
>
> venture capital funding
>
> venture capital firms and exit strategy
>
> LLC vs. corporate structure for start-ups
>
> initial public offering

Targeted groups for this training include (1) students interested in working in start-up companies or managing technology transfer offices; (2) entrepreneurs currently engaged in start-ups; and (3) entrepreneurial faculty.

In sum, universities nationwide have played a major role in transferring their technologies and knowledge to the development of new products and businesses. Although this trend has been successful, there are important areas where improvement is necessary if technology commercialization is to succeed in the long run. Technology transfer offices and start-up companies based on inventions at university laboratories are often managed and operated by staff without sufficient skills in business, law, finance, marketing, and human resource management. For these operations to succeed, they need skilled managers in addition to innovative technology (Kotkin 2004).

# Necessary Regional Infrastructure for a Successful Technology Transfer Strategy

An environment conducive to technology transfer should have the following:

one or more major research universities;

university technology transfer offices that actively support licensing technology to start-ups as well as established companies;

incubator facilities;

appropriate, affordable facilities;

local early-stage venture capital;

knowledgeable service providers; and

a pool of capable entrepreneurs to manage life science and other technology start-ups.

In the next section, we focus on the St. Louis region and examine whether these necessary factors are present for a successful technology transfer environment.

# The St. Louis Experience: A Fertile Growth Region for the Biotechnology Industry

In the early 1990s, the long-term outlook for economic growth in the St. Louis region was becoming dim. Although St. Louis's academic research centers have long been a source of pride for the region, it was apparent that much of the top talent developed by these institutions was escaping to progressive metropolitan areas such as Boston and San Francisco. It was apparent, too, that the region's economic base was slipping as manufacturing jobs were steadily replaced by lower paying retail service jobs. St. Louis also began to document a record number of office and industrial space vacancies. Other metropolitan areas had responded to similar prospects by staking claims on the Internet boom. Civic leaders here assessed the region's existing assets—world-renowned life science research centers and medical facilities—and determined that St. Louis already possessed a basic nutrient needed to grow biotech enterprises. The other vital nutrients, an entrepreneurial infrastructure and a steady stream of investment capital, were actively cultivated in order to turn the region into the BioBelt, or a major life sciences hub. In less than a decade, successful start-up companies such as Quick Study Radiology and Stereotaxis became proof that St. Louis has become fertile ground for the growth of biotech companies.

The remainder of this chapter will examine the successive phases of business development and the extensive network of support that the St. Louis region offers at each phase to ensure that a biotech company will emerge and thrive. First, the region boasts top-tier academic and independent research centers where biotech entrepreneurs can explore the initial concept for a product. Second, the region offers four business incubators with another in development—three of which cater exclusively to science-based companies—that provide start-up companies access to services and facilities that might not otherwise be available. Third, the venture capital needed to fund a start-up's expansion and development in the incubator phase and beyond has become more plentiful thanks to the success of other St. Louis-based start-ups. Fourth, the region is developing post-incubator or "graduate" facilities to provide biotech companies further opportunity to develop products and distribution strategies. Finally, when a biotech company has fully developed, the region offers a specialized full-scale manufacturing space where the company will become a co-tenant with a diverse aggregation of other fully developed science and technology corporations.

# Research Universities and Independent Research Centers: The First Stage of Biotechnology Business Development in the St. Louis Region

The model for a successful technology transfer-based business involves discrete stages, beginning with academic discovery and ending with full-scale manufacturing of a product. Even the most successful technology transfer businesses are driven by a single strong idea that flows from academic research. Such research is therefore critical to the development of a local economy of technology transfer–based businesses. St. Louis has a wide variety of strong research institutions, both university based and independent, which places it in an excellent position to spawn a large number of start-up companies.

Washington University in St. Louis is a world-renowned research university. During FY 2004, the university received $533 million in research support money. The university also ranks fourth among all educational institutions receiving support from the NIH. Washington University is home to the following research centers and institutes, among others: the Genome Sequencing Center, Aerospace Research and Education Center, Center for the Application of Information Technology, Center for BioCybernetics and Intelligent Systems, Computer Communications Research Center, McDonnell Center for the Space Sciences, and Siteman Cancer Center. The School of Medicine, considered one of the best in the nation, is a partner in the Midwest Regional Center of Excellence for Biodefense and Emerging Infectious Diseases Research with Saint Louis University, Case Western Reserve University, University of Missouri–Columbia, and Midwest Research Institute of Kansas City. The university operates a full-time Office of Technology Management to assist members of the university community in transferring technology to private companies. That office also administers the Bear Cub Fund, which supports student and faculty research intended to serve as a foundation for a start-up company, such as proof-of-concept research, in the university research and pre-incubator phase.

Saint Louis University is another highly respected academic institution dedicated to quality research. As part of that commitment, the university recently broke ground on the largest research center in its history, a new $80 million facility on South Grand Boulevard, adjacent to the Health Sciences Center at Saint Louis University, which is composed of four schools, three centers, one hospital, and a practicing physicians group. The center will focus its research on cancer, molecular and structural biology, cardiovascular and pulmonary disease, infectious diseases and biodefense, neurosciences and aging, and liver disease. The Vaccine Evaluation Unit is one of only eleven research centers nationwide chosen by the NIH for sponsored research to find an AIDS vaccine. Saint Louis University also is home to the Institute for Molecular Virology and is a partner in the Midwest Regional Center of Excellence for Biodefense and Emerging Infectious Diseases Research. The Technology Transfer Office, recently renamed the Office of Innovation and Intellectual Property, was established in 1998 to aid university researchers in patent applications and to administer the office's Proof-of-Concept Fund, which allows university researchers to conduct critical experiments or to build a prototype for a product that may be commercialized.

The University of Missouri–St. Louis is yet another leading research university located in the St. Louis area, with more than 1,000 full-time faculty and research staff and nearly 16,000 students. The university houses a number of highly regarded research centers: the Center for Molecular Electronics, Center for Neurodynamics, Center for High Performance Computing, and the International Center for Tropical Ecology, which is operated in conjunction with the Missouri Botanical Garden, the Saint Louis Zoo, and numerous foreign universities and research centers. The University of Missouri–St. Louis is also highly engaged in technology transfer, having established the Center for Emerging Technologies life sciences incubator in 1995, which is discussed later in this chapter.

In addition to three excellent research universities,[1] St. Louis is home to a number of independent research centers. The Missouri Botanical Garden is one of the world's top botanical research and conservation institutions, employing dozens of Ph.D. researchers in the plant sciences fields. The Garden's partnership with the University of Missouri–St. Louis to form the International Center for Tropical Ecology has produced the highest concentration of tropical biologists in the United States. The Garden has substantial research assets, including the Herbarium, plant DNA bank, library and archives, and TROPICOS, the world's largest database of plant information.

The St. Louis region is also home to the Donald Danforth Plant Science Center. The center's research teams work toward the goal of improving human health and nutrition and increasing agricultural production to create a sustainable food supply. To achieve these goals, the Center has partnered with a group of institutions to create the Danforth Center Alliance, composed of the Danforth Plant Science Center, University of Missouri–Columbia, University of Illinois at Urbana-

---

[1] Webster University, Maryville University, Fontbonne University, and others also contribute significantly to the amount of scientific research in the region and supply the St. Louis area with a high-quality scientific labor force.

Champaign, Missouri Botanical Garden, Purdue University, and Washington University in St. Louis. The center has also partnered with other universities in jointly hiring scientists (e.g., UM–St. Louis). The Danforth Plant Science Center's state-of-the-art 150,000-square-foot facility includes fifteen research suites with laboratory support, fourteen greenhouses, thirty-two individual growth chambers, and nineteen custom-designed growth rooms. The center was also the recipient of a major grant of $3.3 million from the Bill and Melinda Gates Foundation to increase the disease resistance and nutritional content of cassava, the primary food crop of sub-Saharan Africa.

The Saint Louis Zoo houses additional life-science research specialists. The primary research focus of the zoo is animal reproduction, with a goal of ensuring continued existence of threatened and endangered species. This includes research in the areas of animal behavior, physiology, endocrinology, and gamete biology. The zoo is also home to the American Zoo and Aquarium Association's Wildlife Contraception Center, the Endangered Species Research Center, the Veterinary Hospital, and a pathology laboratory.

**Greenhouses at the Donald Danforth Plant Science Center.**
**Photo courtesy of the Donald Danforth Plant Science Center.**

St. Louis's broad base of academic research at universities and independent research centers provides an excellent platform for the development of technology transfer–based businesses and also makes St. Louis attractive to venture capitalists. The availability of local talent produced by the region's academic institutions and drawn to the region by its life science industry assets is a key factor in the decision to bring venture capital to a region. The facts illustrate that St. Louis has already been able to capitalize on these substantial assets. In 2002, the last year for which data are available, investment in local academic research was up by 57 percent, ranking St. Louis third in the nation for increases in academic research funding. That same year, local universities granted more than three thousand biotech degrees. In 2002, the region ranked in the top 20 out of 371 metropolitan areas in the number of biotech businesses.

As these statistics show, St. Louis is primed to translate its success in research to success in industry through technology transfer–based businesses. To help ensure that this transition is realized, in 2000 Civic Progress and the St. Louis Regional Chamber and Growth Association created the Coalition for Plant and Life Sciences. The Coalition, a group consisting of many of the region's top business, civic, academic, and research leaders headed by Dr. William H. Danforth, oversees the implementation of a plan to position St. Louis as an international center for biomedical and plant sciences business.

# St. Louis Incubators: Fostering Growth from Innovation to Business

When investigators prepare to conduct research and product development outside of the university, they often apply for admission to an incubator to assist them with their business growth. Incubators provide fledgling companies with the resources they need to develop their product until they have the financial capability, business skills, and facilities to operate independently. While in an incubator, newly founded science or technology companies receive access to facilities, services, and business development counseling. The St. Louis region is home to four incubators: the Nidus Center for Scientific Enterprise, Technology Entrepreneur

Center, Center for Emerging Technologies, and St. Louis Enterprise Centers. The first three particularly cater to new companies in science and information technology. An information technology incubator also is currently under development at the UM–St. Louis campus, which will house ten to twelve start-ups and a high-performance computing center. With the diverse focus areas of these incubators, St. Louis is prepared to meet the research and development needs of almost any start-up science and technology company.

The Nidus Center for Scientific Enterprise, located near the Monsanto corporate campus in Creve Coeur, Missouri, aims to speed marketing of innovative ideas in all the life sciences. However, Nidus caters particularly to entrepreneurs who are refining and preparing new plant science technologies for market. Its 40,000-square-foot building currently is home to seven new plant and life science companies. Nidus clients include Akermin, Inc., a company engaged in the development of biofuel cell technology, and Graphic Surgery, LLC, a medical service company developing a medical information system to decrease surgical malpractice liability and increase surgeon productivity.

Nidus provides clients with all the resources they need to eventually become successful, independent business entities. Clients receive on-site access to the latest data networking technology, hazardous/biohazard waste removal, federal licensing for radioactive materials use, scientific photographic film developing, and a growth chamber. Nidus also gives clients the business support they need to eventually stand on their own in the St. Louis market. Clients attend seminars on business-plan development and business expansion. They also receive coaching from the Center's CEO and access to start-up capital sources.

Another St. Louis life sciences incubator, the Center for Emerging Technologies (CET), assists companies developing products from numerous areas of biotechnology. An affiliate of the University of Missouri–St. Louis, CET is located near the Washington University School of Medicine and the Saint Louis University campus. Under the direction of the president and CEO, the Center's tenant companies develop cutting-edge technology with significant market potential. One tenant, BioSynthema, develops radiopharmaceuticals for the diagnosis and treatment of cancer. Another successful tenant, Auxeris Therapeutics, Inc., is developing breakthrough medicines to treat a broad range of bone diseases including the first oral bone anabolic drug to prevent and treat osteoporosis and a mechanism-based antiresorptive to prevent bone metastases. Perhaps the most prominent tenant success story is that of Stereotaxis, a company that developed a revolutionary surgical device combining magnetic guidance with advanced radiological imaging techniques. Stereotaxis has successfully completed its stay at CET and has leased development and production space in the Center of Research, Technology, and Entrepreneurial eXchange (CORTEX) biotech building, located a short distance from CET and completed in 2005.

**The Center for Emerging Technologies operates a two-building complex totaling 92,000 square feet. Photo by Debbie Franke. ©Debbie Franke Photography, Inc.**

The success of CET is known both locally and nationally. In 2003, the National Business Incubation Association named CET one of the top ten incubators in the country. The association also ranked CET first in the country in average revenue growth. As of June 30, 2005, CET had raised $479 million in venture capital investments, corporate contracts, and research grants.

While the Nidus and CET incubators are geared toward developing life science entrepreneurs, St. Louis offers business incubation facilities for other industries, from retail at the St. Louis Enterprise Centers to information technology at the UM–St. Louis technology incubator slated to open in early 2007 and the currently operating Technology Entrepreneur Center (TEC). The TEC, located in downtown St. Louis in the Bandwidth Exchange Building, provides start-up services to new information and communications technology companies. Under the direction of president Jim Brasunas, TEC's five current clients are developing technology that the center believes will spur economic development and job creation in the St. Louis area. For example, Minute Guard LLC, one of TEC's developing companies, has created the first proactive cellular management tool for eliminating cellular overage expenses. The company is developing an online service that alerts registered users via text messaging before they go over their allotted monthly minutes.

# Venture Capital and Its Role in St. Louis's Biotechnology Business Development

Funding becomes a pressing concern in the incubator stage of development because most start-ups lack the collateral needed to secure bank loans, and the wait for research efforts to translate into revenue might be years. The start-up relies mostly on the precocity and patience of angel and venture capital investors to see the company through these "lean" years. Venture capital is a risky investment of equity (often private and public) in a start-up that is usually long on potential but short on capital.

St. Louis welcomed a steady stream of venture capital investments between 2000 and 2005 with over $800 million in investments in St. Louis companies during that time. In 2004, firms invested more than $120 million in the city's science and technology companies—an increase of almost 25 percent over the previous year. Participants from eight states and three countries contributed to this influx of venture capital. St. Louis–based funds alone currently manage almost $830 million in venture capital. A start-up in St. Louis can now enjoy the benefits of this surge of venture capital thanks in substantial measure to large venture capital funds including Vectis Life Sciences, local funds such as Prolog Ventures and Oakwood Medical Investors, and a strong network of regional support.

As a large-scale fund-of-funds program, the $81.5 million Vectis Life Sciences Fund I has drawn the attention of investors nationwide. Vectis I will invest in smaller funds which will in turn invest in local biotech start-ups. Large out-of-state firms are often reluctant to invest in distant start-ups due to the difficulty of overseeing the management of the company's day-to-day operations. Peter Brooke, a venture capital expert credited with turning Boston into a science and technology hub, developed Vectis I with the aim of connecting local venture capital firms like Prolog Ventures and Oakwood Medical Investors with large out-of-state investors. The fund-of-funds arrangement decreases risk for out-of-state investors by increasing the total number of investors. Moreover, the out-of-state firms can rely on local investors to assist in the management of the start-up.

Prolog Ventures and Oakwood Medical Investors are examples of smaller in-state funds that strive to localize venture capital. Prolog Ventures invests in biotech and related information technology start-ups already located in Missouri or those with plans to relocate to the area. With $100 million already under management, Prolog closed on a $66 million fund in June 2005. In addition to the almost $18 million received from Vectis I, Prolog's sources of funding include Washington University, public pension funds, and private individuals. Through four rounds of funding, Oakwood Medical Investors has raised approximately $78 million for the biotech industry—most of which will be invested in the St. Louis area. Of those out-of-state biotech companies that receive venture capital from Oakwood, many have plans to move some of their operations to St. Louis.

To further increase St. Louis's visibility in the venture capital community, the representatives of the region participate in annual investment forums like the InvestMidwest Venture Capital Forum and BIO's MidAmerica Venture Forum, which introduce venture capitalists to science and technology start-ups from the region. In 2004, St. Louis hosted the MidAmerica Venture Forum. Twenty-one life science companies based in St. Louis were given an opportunity to present their business plans to a collection of investment firms. In 2005, seventy venture capital firms attended the InvestMidwest forum held that year in Kansas City. The forum showcased presentations from thirty companies—nine of which were St. Louis start-ups.

Financial incentives from federal and state government sources also encourage venture capitalists to invest in the local industry. The New Markets Tax Credit program offers tax credits to firms who invest in targeted neighborhoods. In 2005, Advantage Capital Partners, a venture capital firm with offices nationwide, received a $50 million tax credit in exchange, in part, for a promise to invest in companies either located in St. Louis or with plans to relocate to the metropolitan area. The State of Missouri also offers a number of programs to encourage investment in the St. Louis region, including the Certified Capital Company (CAPCO) tax credit program, the Cultural Facility Revenue Bonds program implemented by the Missouri Development Finance Board, and the Community Development Block Grant Action Fund Loan and the Small Business Incubator Tax Credit programs designed to encourage small-business development. Additionally, the state treasurer has assigned a task force the mission of exploring the possibility of involving the state's largest pension funds—the Missouri State Employees' Retirement System and the Public School Retirement System—in future rounds of venture capital funding.

In addition to these vital financial services, the St. Louis region also offers high-quality legal services at a bargain rate compared to firms on either coast or in larger midwestern metropolitan areas like Chicago. Legal services in St. Louis are becoming tailored to meet the specific needs of the biotech industry. One of the region's largest firms has estimated that up to 20 percent of its business is biotech related. The region also offers other options to a start-up that might not be able to afford the services of a large firm. For example, some local law firms will offer to share patent application costs. Additionally, area start-ups can take advantage of the legal services offered by the Intellectual Property and Business Formation Legal Clinic at Washington University.

The region's participation in annual investment forums, the array of federal and state incentives, and the availability of bargain-rate ancillary services continue to improve funding options for St. Louis biotech firms with little start-up capital. By comparing St. Louis to Boston in the 1970s, Peter Brooke predicted that St. Louis is on the verge of becoming the favorite target of venture capitalists. According to Brooke, St. Louis has "all the raw materials to become a great region for venture capital investment" (Imbs 2005).

# Post-Incubator Stage of Business Development: CORTEX and the Emergence of "Graduate" and Multi-Tenant Facilities in St. Louis

The founding, permanent members of the Center of Research, Technology, and Entrepreneurial eXchange (CORTEX) are Washington University in St. Louis, Saint Louis University, the University of Missouri–St. Louis, BJC HealthCare, and the Missouri Botanical Garden. Led by CEO John Dubinsky, CORTEX aims to promote, advocate, and assure the St. Louis region's economic progress as a center of biomedical research, education, business, and industry. Through acquiring property and establishing land-use controls, CORTEX plans to transform midtown St. Louis into an urban technology corridor with facilities for biomedical and other advanced technology companies that have developed beyond the incubator stage.[2]

After completing the incubator stage, the next phase of development for emerging biotech companies is the move into shared "graduate" or multi-tenant space. In this space, the companies have access to physical systems that enable them to complete their business and research development. In St. Louis, CORTEX has constructed a state-of-the-art, $36 million building to provide such space to companies that are ready to move out of incubators.

The CORTEX development is situated in the area of the city historically known by many as "Technopolis." Within this large area, CORTEX has identified two major sectors to serve as centers for the development of facilities for St. Louis biotech companies in various stages of business development. These areas will hopefully become home to a diverse array of research and commercial technology enterprises. However, CORTEX, as a Missouri not-for-profit corporation, is working to stimulate further development of its two designated areas as a life and plant science development, sales, and distribution center.

---

[2] Of course, without the timely cooperation of local government and elected officials for zoning issues and building and occupancy permits, development of the biotech industry in St. Louis would be almost impossible.

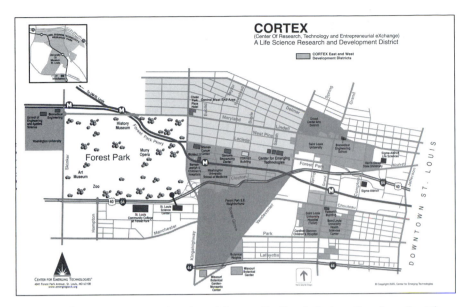

Map of CORTEX, a region in midtown St. Louis being developed with
facilities for biotech companies that have grown beyond the incubator stage.
Image courtesy of Center for Emerging Technologies.

# Research Parks in the St. Louis Region

While CORTEX plans to offer facilities for companies that have
completed the development phases and are ready for their own
independent, full-scale manufacturing space, such facilities currently exist
in the St. Louis region in the Missouri Research Park (MRP). The park is
owned by and under the direction of the University of Missouri System.
Since its beginning in 1989, MRP has developed in St. Charles County
between the Missouri River and Highway 94. A $5 million Highway 40
overpass was constructed to connect the park to its new entrance on
Technology Drive.

The buildings offered for lease in the 750-acre Missouri Research Park
are designed to accommodate a diverse array of science and technology
companies. Some of the park's tenant companies market key developments
for the aerospace and automotive industries. For example, Zoltek
Corporation develops and produces high-purity carbon fibers used in both
aerospace and automotive manufacture. Other tenants develop and

manufacture products geared toward the life science industry. Linco Research, Inc., develops and manufactures reagents for diabetes research from its facilities in the park. Several large well-known companies conduct research and manufacture products from facilities in the park, including Nike IHM, Inc., an independently run subsidiary of sports giant Nike, Inc. From MRP, Nike IHM produces polyurethane materials with uses spanning automotive airbags and sporting goods to medical therapy bladders and mattresses. Nearby, the National Weather Service has a regional forecasting center and Doppler radar research facility in the park.

MRP also offers numerous amenities to add to the comfort of the residents and their current and potential clients. The park has a golf course and country club as well as hiking and walking trails. Its hotel, the Wingate, includes reception and conference facilities.

To supplement the space offered at the Missouri Research Park, the University of Missouri–St. Louis is developing a one-hundred-acre business, technology, and research park adjacent to the university's north campus next to Interstate 70. In the early planning stages, the research park had already attracted substantial interest from both small ventures and established Fortune 500 companies. Express Scripts, which is one of the largest pharmacy-benefit management companies in North America, will build its new corporate headquarters at UM–St. Louis's research park with occupancy expected in early 2007. The company will be the highest-ranking Fortune 500 company with its corporate headquarters on a university campus.

# A Case Study: Stereotaxis

A biotech start-up would be well served by following the example of St. Louis–based Stereotaxis. Stereotaxis began in 1990 with only two employees and a concept. Since arriving in St. Louis, Stereotaxis has expanded its operations, simplified its technology, and garnered national attention for the return enjoyed by the company's investors.

## The Concept

Stereotaxis developed a computer-enhanced surgical system that employs small magnets to guide instruments during neuro- and cardiosurgery. The device enables physicians to perform life-saving procedures with a high level of precision and a minimum of invasiveness.

## Early-Stage Research and Development

In 1994, Stereotaxis relocated to St. Louis. The company's two employees opened an office at Barnes-Jewish Hospital and established a relationship with the neurosurgery department at Washington University. Local and out-of-state investors teamed together to prop up Stereotaxis in the early days with $5 million of venture capital. Local investors included Oakwood Medical Investors and Barnes-Jewish Hospital. Out-of-state investors included California-based Sanderling Ventures and Alafi Capital.

Local investors are drawn to start-ups like Stereotaxis because the concept suggests the potential of a significant return. Here, Stereotaxis addressed (1) hospitals' desire to attract new patients by offering a state-of-the-art surgical device; (2) physicians' efforts to improve their patients' outcomes; and (3) patients' demands for less invasive procedures.

## Incubator Space

Stereotaxis moved to the Center for Emerging Technologies incubator in 1998. Stereotaxis received more than $18 million in venture capital to help finance clinical trials, company scale-up, and operations. St. Louis–based investors Advantage Capital Partners and Gateway Associates were heavily involved in this round of funding.

Advantage Capital Partners invests in high-growth companies like Stereotaxis and other projects such as real estate using unique structured-finance investment vehicles. These investment vehicles make use of various federal and state economic development incentives, including the federal New Markets Tax Credit program, Certified Capital Company (CAPCO) programs, various state tax credit programs, and federal loan guarantee programs.

Venture capital funneled in from out-of-state sources such as California-based firms Ampersand and Alafi Capital Company, and Boston-based firm Advent International. From its local and out-of-state sources, Stereotaxis raised approximately $130 million in venture capital prior to 2004.

The technology improved. The device is now less than half the size of the prototype, and the controlling mechanism has been simplified to resemble a video-game controller. The improvements have opened the possibility of applications in other surgical procedures aside from brain and heart surgery.

## "Graduate" Space

Stereotaxis is now the largest company at the CET, with more than one hundred employees. The company has leased space in the new CORTEX building. The lease at CORTEX, which includes a provision for expansion, will run for ten years beginning in late 2005.

**Results**

In 2004, Stereotaxis went public. The company sold 5.5 million shares at $8 per share and collected $48 million.

# Conclusion: The Region and Industry Grow Together

Over the course of the last decade, since the goal of becoming the BioBelt was first formulated, St. Louis has fostered a symbiotic relationship with the biotech industry. The region's entrepreneurial infrastructure continues to facilitate the growth of successful companies like Stereotaxis, and the region's universities continue to train some of the industry's top talent. In exchange, the long-term economic outlook for St. Louis has improved. St. Louis is now able to retain more of its research talent in high-skill, high-pay biotech jobs and has experienced an increase in the amount of investment capital flowing into the region. As the biotech industry grows to rely on the region's research centers, business incubators, and post-incubator support facilities, St. Louis continues to cultivate the local soil so that biotech companies of any size and at any phase of development can thrive. Consequently, the development, additional employment, and overall economic impact of each phase of the business incubator development process have generated additional development on a mixed-use scale in surrounding neighborhoods.

**Acknowledgments**

The authors thank Matt Aplington, Charla Scott, and William Rearden, summer interns at the Stolar Partnership, for their participation in the research and drafting for this manuscript; and Marcia Mellitz at the Center for Emerging Technologies and Tamara Kratochvil at UM–St. Louis for their valuable editorial assistance. This work was supported in part by the U.S. Army Research Development and Engineering Command Acquisition Center. The content of the information does not necessarily reflect the position or the policy of the federal government, and no official endorsement should be inferred.

**References**

Allan, Michael F. "The Review of Best Practices in University Technology Licensing Offices." *The Journal of the Association of University Technology Managers* 13 (2001).

Arshadi, Nasser, and Gordon V. Karels. *Modern Financial Intermediaries and Markets.* Upper Saddle River, NJ: Prentice Hall, 1997.

Bremer, Howard W. "University Technology Transfer Evolution and Revolution." Presentation, Fiftieth Anniversary of the Council on Government Relations, Washington, DC, November 3, 2003.

Gates, Edward R., and Michael N. Rader. "Disentangling Inventorship." *The Journal of the Association of University Technology Managers* 13 (2001).

Imbs, Christine. "Biotechnology in St. Louis: Stepping Out of Boston's Shadow?" *St. Louis Commerce Magazine,* June 2005. http://www.stlcommercemagazine.com/archives/june2005/biotechnology.html.

Jamison, Douglas W., and Christina Jansen. "Technology Transfer and Economic Growth." *The Journal of the Association of University Technology Managers* 12 (2000).

Kotkin, Joel. "The Corps of Rediscovery: St. Louis in the 21st Century." *Regional Talent Project Report* prepared for the St. Louis Regional Chamber and Growth Association and Greater St. Louis Economic Development Council, St. Louis, Spring 2004.

Pressman, Lori. "What Is Known and Knowable About the Economic Impact of University Technology Transfer Programs?" Presentation, NASULGC Annual Meeting, Chicago, 2002.

Sample, Steven B. "Innovation and Technology Transfer in Universities." Presentation, California Public Affairs Forum of the California Council on Science and Technology, Stanford Research Institute, Menlo Park, CA, December 3, 2001.

U.S. Patent and Trademark Office. "General Information Concerning Patents." http://www.uspto.gov/web/offices/pac/doc/general/index.html#ptsc (accessed January 2006).

Weber, Luc E., and James J. Duderstadt, eds. *Reinventing the Research University.* London: Economica, 2004.

Winner, Ellen P. "Federally Registered Trademarks Add Value to Technology." *The Journal of the Association of University Technology Managers* 11 (1999).

# Chapter 4

# Sports Under the Arch: St. Louis Teams, Venues, and Public Support

**Donald Phares**

Why has St. Louis invested in sports assets? During the 1990s St. Louis was in the position of losing the two professional teams still in town, the baseball Cardinals and the Blues hockey team, and also trying to attract a football team back to the city. To meet the challenge, both public and private community resources were focused along several fronts. The first front was attention to keeping the Blues in St. Louis. Their home, the St. Louis Arena, was showing its age, and ownership had been very unstable—thus raising the strong possibility of it moving. Second, a commitment was made to building a new football stadium and to enticing a team to replace the football Cardinals, who left the city in 1988. This became a major public/private sports venture, arguably one of the largest in St. Louis history. Finally, at the end of 1995, to great public dismay, Anheuser-Busch announced it was selling the baseball Cardinals after more than four decades of ownership. Maintaining local control and keeping baseball became a prime concern.

The St. Louis sports community was suddenly being challenged on many fronts. The age of the existing stadium has been an issue with the new owners. In order to maintain St. Louis's status as a sports city, and after numerous financial iterations, a new, primarily privately funded ballpark is being constructed as home to the Cardinals.

A second facet of sports investment was related to the sports "image" of St. Louis. Baseball has been the sports lifeblood of the city. Hockey has been an integral part of St. Louis sports for almost thirty years. Any danger to either of these drew strong local reaction. Attracting football became a rallying point, perhaps breathing more fervor into the community than any issue in a long time. But the support and commitment was more than just for sports—it became an issue of the public perception of St. Louis. St. Louis had been receiving bad press for decades. Many in the city political structure and the corporate power elite appreciated the PR value of sports and pushed hard for the investment in sports to have a significant return. Sports was clearly considered a major asset for St. Louis.

The third facet of sports investment relates to rebuilding the downtown. There had been talk for a long while, even prior to the football Cardinals leaving, of expanding the Cervantes Convention Center to include a domed stadium. Such a facility could house a football team, keep St. Louis competitive with the rapidly evolving national venue market, and greatly expand the capacity of the convention complex. The city would be investing in the infrastructure necessary to link its sports, tourism, and recreation economic base. It could move up the convention-city pecking order to a new level. Football provided the prime impetus and adrenaline for the domed stadium expansion. The strategy was "build and they shall come."

It is difficult, however, to characterize what St. Louis has done as part of a clearly articulated overall strategy. In many respects its response resembles more a reaction to a series of crises: Keep the Blues in town by providing a new home and stabilizing ownership; by no means allow the baseball Cardinals to leave town; get a new football team but first build a stadium. The $390 million baseball park begun in 2005 attests to the desire to make certain the Cardinals are not lured away.

# Sports Teams in St. Louis

St. Louis has a long and rich history in professional sports. It has been the home to every major type of professional sport including basketball, baseball, football, and hockey, as well as indoor soccer, arena football, and roller hockey. At present, it is home base for the Cardinals, Rams, and Blues. A professional basketball team, the Hawks, played here between 1955 and 1968; they later moved due to declining attendance. The Spirits of St. Louis played two years, a casualty of the ABA-NBA merger. While there have been attempts to attract a new basketball franchise, nothing has materialized.

## Baseball

St. Louis's long-term success with sports has been baseball. It has been a die-hard baseball town for well over a century. In fact, for more than fifty years St. Louis was home to two teams, the Browns and the Cardinals. Between 1902 and 1953 the Browns shared Sportsman's Park with the Cardinals. Perhaps one of the most notable events in St. Louis baseball history occurred in 1944 when the Cardinals and the Browns played each other in the so-called streetcar world series, won by the Cardinals. The Browns left town in 1953.

The Cardinals have played in St. Louis since 1892, using several venues. They began their career playing in Robison Field and later moved to Sportsman's Park. In 1953 the team was purchased by August "Gussie" Busch, for the brewery bearing his name. The Cardinals played in "old" Busch Stadium (Sportsman's Park) until a new stadium was completed downtown in 1966. The new stadium was officially called Busch Stadium.

Crowd gathered around St. Louis Cardinals during the pregame warm-ups
at Robison Field. Photograph by William H. Trefts Jr.
MHS Photographs and Prints.

A shock was delivered to the community in 1995, when the brewery announced plans to sell the Cardinals. Baseball no longer fit in the brewery's corporate plans; this marked the formal end of the "beer and baseball" era but not the loss of the team. Every effort was made to structure the sale of the Cardinals so that the team would stay. Toward this end, the team, the stadium, and the parking garages were bundled as a package deal, ensuring that the team would not be sold separately and moved from St. Louis. A group composed primarily of St. Louis locals bought all three for $150 million.

Keeping baseball in St. Louis clearly has been a goal of both previous owners and the new owners. This is fortunate, because the loss of the Cardinals might well have meant the demise of baseball in St. Louis, a city that has been linked to baseball history for over a century. In the intensely competitive sports marketplace, it was unlikely that St. Louis could have lured a new franchise without a new stadium. While in excellent condition and with an adequate seating capacity of over 50,000, Busch Stadium still was thirty years old. A new team, having a clear advantage in the sports relocation frenzy, would have demanded a new venue. At that time, given the huge amount of money spent on the new Trans World Dome and Kiel Center, public and private resources and community willingness to give any more to sports had been tapped out.

**Football**

The football Cardinals moved to St. Louis from Chicago in 1960. Between 1960 and 1965 they played at Sportsman's Park. In 1966 they moved to Busch Stadium. As will be discussed later, this downtown stadium became the focal point for a major renewal program.

The Cardinals played at Busch Stadium until 1988 when the owner, Bill Bidwill, moved the team to Phoenix. At this point antagonism between the team and the St. Louis community was so high that a new football stadium was not in the cards. The Cardinals left, and St. Louis was without football for the first time in more than twenty-five years.

The football void was filled almost immediately by a succession of groups focused on getting a new team. As they worked with the community, a decision was made to build a new stadium and use it to lure a team. Construction began in early 1993 without a team in sight. The sequence of events and participants was convoluted and unfolded between 1990 and 1995. When St. Louis lost its bid for an expansion team in 1993, FANS Inc. stepped into the fray. After lengthy and complex legal and political machinations, former U.S. senator Thomas Eagleton was able to resolve the outstanding issues and entice the Los Angeles Rams to relocate. Because of his experience and stature in the community, Senator Eagleton was uniquely qualified to link the three key elements for getting football back to St. Louis: the lease for the already-built new stadium, the necessary financial resources to attract a team, and a team willing to move. Football had returned! The thirty-year price tag was $720 million in public funds for the stadium plus another $200 million in private funds to attract the Rams. A clear payoff to the community has been the Rams' participation in two Super Bowls and their Super Bowl victory in 2000.

## Hockey

Professional hockey has been played in St. Louis since 1967 when Sidney Solomon purchased the financially troubled St. Louis Arena after being promised an NHL franchise, which turned out to be the Blues. In 1977 he sold the team to St. Louis–based Ralston Purina. For the next fourteen years the Blues skated on thin financial ice. After reportedly losing millions of dollars, Ralston tried to sell the team to Civic Progress, an organization of select local corporate leaders. They declined, and the team nearly went bankrupt. Finally, the Blues and the Arena were purchased by a non-local investor, Harry Ornest, for a "fire-sale" price. In 1986, after trying unsuccessfully to move the team to Canada, Ornest sold the team to a local group, Kiel Center Partners, which was later known as Clark Enterprises. The Arena was bought by the City of St. Louis, and for the first time ownership of the team and the venue was split. The Blues played at the Arena until 1994, when they moved into the new Kiel Center, which had been developed by the Blues' owners in conjunction with the City of St. Louis.

The Blues were purchased from Clark Enterprises by the Lauries for $100 million in 1999 along with long-term lease rights to the Kiel Center. The name of the venue was changed to the Savvis Center. In 2005, after years and tens of millions in losses, the owners announced their intention to sell the team and lease rights. There are efforts under way to keep the team in St. Louis, but once again there is a threat the Blues will leave.

## Basketball

St. Louis's basketball experience was relatively brief, spanning the years from 1955 to 1968. Basketball has not been a local sports success story. The Hawks moved to the city in 1955 from Milwaukee, where they had played since 1949. The Hawks' stay was characterized by a general lack of interest from the community, and their last few years were marked by a precipitous drop in attendance. The economics of the situation eventually forced the movement of the team in 1968. One other team played in St. Louis from 1974 to 1976, the Spirits, but they did not survive the ABA-NBA merger. Bill Laurie, owner of the Blues, made several unsuccessful attempts to bring a team to St. Louis that could share the Savvis Center, and its cost, with the Blues.

# Sports Venues in St. Louis

St. Louis teams have used numerous facilities over the years. To respond to the intense competition in the sports marketplace, two new facilities were opened in the 1990s and a new baseball stadium was completed in 2006. Like other cities, St. Louis faces a new era, where the economic development and viability of downtown is more dependent on leisure and tourism. The downtown urban economic engine is now fueled much more by sports teams and their venues, which can also accommodate large conventions or exhibits. A contribution to this new wave of economic expansion has been public support to finance venues and infrastructure; it has assumed several forms.

The following narrative looks at each of the major sports venues in St. Louis, how they came into existence, their teams, and the role of public support. It involves leases, subleases, and sub-subleases; direct public and private funding; both local and federal tax breaks; use of eminent domain; public bonding authority; and other public concessions such as non-compete clauses and deed restrictions. Money has played a major role, but other public concessions have been of consequence as well.

### A Snapshot of St. Louis Sports

A noteworthy aspect of St. Louis's venue development is that of the two new facilities built in the 1990s, one is virtually 100 percent publicly financed (the Edward Jones Dome) and the other was funded primarily with private money (the new Cardinals ballpark). Of the three other, older sports facilities, one always has been private (Busch Stadium), one was built as a municipal auditorium (Kiel Auditorium), and one (the Arena) was privately developed but at the end of its use for professional sports became unusable City property. St. Louis offers a case study for diverse experience in venue development across the public-private continuum.

The history of the four existing St. Louis venues differs significantly. The Trans World Dome (now Edward Jones Dome) opened in 1995. The Kiel Center opened in late 1994 in the same spot as the old municipal facility, Kiel Auditorium, which had opened in 1934. Busch Stadium was completed in 1966 as the focal component of a massive downtown renewal effort. Here is a near-forty-year-old example of sports playing a central role in urban renewal for a city that had experienced significant economic deterioration and loss of residents and commerce. However, Busch Stadium was almost entirely developed with private funds, whereas today's venues depend on extensive public investment. Finally there is the St. Louis Arena. This facility opened in 1929, but it was not until 1967 that it became home to a professional sports team.

**Table 1. St. Louis Venues and Teams**

| Venue | Teams | Sport |
|---|---|---|
| Sportsman's Park (1876) | St. Louis Cardinals | Baseball |
| (it has had various names) | St. Louis Browns | Baseball |
| | St. Louis Cardinals | Football |
| St. Louis Arena (1929) | St. Louis Blues | Hockey |
| (demolished in 1999) | Spirits of St. Louis | Basketball |
| Kiel Auditorium (1934) | St. Louis Hawks | Basketball |
| (demolished in 1992 for the Kiel Center) | | |
| Busch Stadium (1966) | St. Louis Cardinals | Baseball |
| | St. Louis Cardinals | Football |
| Kiel Center (1994) | St. Louis Blues | Hockey |
| (now the Savvis Center) | St. Louis Ambush | Indoor soccer |
| | St. Louis Stampede | Arena football |
| | St. Louis Vipers | Roller hockey |
| Trans World Dome (1995) | St. Louis Rams | Football |
| (now the Edward Jones Dome) | | |
| Busch Stadium (2006) | St. Louis Cardinals | Baseball |

## Football Returns: The Trans World Dome

A major addition to St. Louis sports venues is the Trans World Dome, now called the Edward Jones Dome, home to the St. Louis Rams.

Building this stadium raised a lot of issues, mostly financial. In a national context, questions about the precedent-setting nature of the financial package to attract the Rams plus the cost of the new stadium reverberated through the football world. How would it affect the bargaining position of other cities that were contemplating building a new stadium and/or attracting a team? Locally, the "staggering" cost of the Rams deal still raised the question, "Was it worth it?" Given the thirty-year, near $1 billion price tag for the Rams plus the Trans World Dome, this question was not without merit.

Let's begin the story with a question asked and then answered by a local sports columnist. All things taken into account, was the Rams acquisition a bargain for St. Louis? In a *St. Louis Post-Dispatch* column, Bernie Miklasz argued yes. He said that the old Arena facility had been used from 1929 to 1994 and housed the Blues for most of their twenty-seven years in St. Louis. When they left the Arena in 1994 they moved into the Kiel Center, which was heavily financed with private funds. The baseball Cardinals used Sportsman's Park until the Anheuser-Busch company put up seed money for construction of a new baseball park in the early 1960s (Miklasz 1995).

**Aerial view of Sportsman's Park, September 15, 1955. Photograph by Ted McCrea, 1955. MHS Photographs and Prints.**

A proposal that was floated in the mid-1980s to invest in a $90 million stadium to retain the football Cardinals, much more conservative than the $300 million Trans World Dome, was "shouted down" (Miklasz 1995, 2). As Miklasz notes: "For decades, St. Louis lagged behind the rest of the nation in sports investment. That inflated the cost of the Rams' contract. St. Louis had to catch up. If anything, the ledger is even." Of St. Louis's three professional sports teams only the football franchise eventually required primarily public funding. "In the context of history, that's a bargain," said Miklasz (1995, 2).

Was his assessment correct? Was it worth the cost? What was the cost? Let's unravel the details of St. Louis's commitment to building the Trans World Dome and enticing the Los Angeles Rams. In 1988 the football Cardinals, attracted by a large financial incentive and promise of a new stadium, moved to Phoenix. After their departure there emerged a void surrounding the return of football to St. Louis. The community, local businesses, and the city all wanted football in town. Into this void moved the NFL Partnership (NFLP). The partnership was headed by Jerry Clinton, the president of Grey Eagle Distributors of St. Louis. Also in the partnership were Fran Murray, who at the time owned 49 percent of the New England Patriots, and Walter Payton, former running back for the Chicago Bears.

Realizing that the stadium issue would not go away, the NFLP became a major driving force behind the expansion of what was then the Cervantes Convention Center, pushing for it to include a state-of-the-art stadium. The rationale was that, when used in conjunction with the existing convention center complex, it would not only house a new team but also increase the City's attractiveness for major conventions, exhibits, and shows. It would move St. Louis up a notch in this competitive and expanding national market.

All attention and zeal were focused on getting a new team; the stadium deal moved forward. It was decided to build a new state-of-the art stadium and then get a team, a strategy that had been used elsewhere.

The NFLP signed a thirty-year lease with the St. Louis Convention and Visitors Commission (CVC), which operates the convention center complex, for use of the new stadium. As a result the NFLP also would get an impressive array of income flows and other concessions, including all income from food, beverages, and concessions on a game day; all income from the sale or rental of luxury boxes; most income from advertising; and all income from club seats. The CVC agreed to manage, operate, and maintain the stadium on game days. This was obtained for a thirty-year fixed annual lease cost of $250,000.

As an integral component of the overall financing plan for the new stadium, a tax on hotel and motel rooms was submitted to St. Louis County voters. The proposal was approved by a two-thirds majority. Proceeds from the County hotel/motel tax were earmarked to pay for its share of stadium construction and maintenance, $6 million per year. The remaining funding for the stadium would come from the City of St. Louis ($6 million) and the State of Missouri ($12 million). This annual funding package would be used to retire the thirty-year construction bonds ($20 million per year) and set up a preservation fund ($4 million per year).

The stadium project's funding represented a first for the St. Louis area in that it linked the city, county, and state in investing in a regional project. This takes on even greater significance for an area in which regional cooperation is scarce and state involvement in such a clearly regional project is minimal. At the time some optimists even argued it set a precedent for greater state involvement in regional projects.

With the lease and financing apparently settled, the issue of who was actually in charge of getting a new football team took on even more import. Disputes within the NFLP led to formation of a new partnership, the Gateway Football Partnership. Gateway came onto the local scene in an attempt to woo an expansion team from the NFL. The NFL delayed its decision, originally scheduled for October, on awarding the two expansion teams. Apparently, the existing lease fiasco with the NFLP had placed a financial cloud over the viability of St. Louis's bid. Much to the shock of St. Louis, the league awarded expansion teams to Charlotte and Jacksonville. St. Louis lost its bid, and many argue this was in large part because the financing for the new team was unclear and colored by the threat of litigation over control of the stadium lease. The Stallions, as the team was to be named, never materialized.

After the failure of the expansion team bid, a new group emerged. FANS Inc. took over the lease rights to the stadium. With considerable effort, FANS Inc. resolved all of the lease and side agreement issues surrounding the original NFLP agreement with CVC. FANS Inc. also managed to lure the Los Angeles Rams to St. Louis with a lucrative deal for the team's owner.

A public entity, the St. Louis Regional Convention and Sports Complex Authority, was established in 1989 by the Missouri legislature to build the stadium as an integral part of the America's Center convention complex.

The Authority issued $258,670,000 in bonds in 1991 and earned an additional $40 million by investing the proceeds until actually used. The Sports Complex Authority is an independent public entity with bipartisan commissioners: five from the state, three from the city, and three from the county. While built by the Sports Complex Authority, the stadium is actually run by the CVC under a lease with the Sports Complex Authority. The Rams in turn sublease the stadium from the CVC.

The stadium will be paid for by taxpayers until the year 2022; the City and County each pay $6 million per year and the State of Missouri pays $12 million. The full cost to pay off the bond indebtedness plus annual maintenance will be some $720 million. Only a small amount of private funds went for actual stadium construction, about $4.2 million from the proceeds of Personal Seat Licenses (PSLs).

As successor to the NFLP and Gateway, FANS Inc., led by former U.S. senator Thomas Eagleton, negotiated with the L.A. Rams to move them here and raised money from local fans to finance the move by using revenue from PSLs. Rams president John Shaw orchestrated the move for the Rams, and in January of 1995 the Sports Complex Authority entered into a relocation agreement with CVC, FANS Inc., and the Rams, to move the Rams here.

The total cost of moving the Rams was estimated to be $191 million. This included, as part of the original $120 million deal, $60 million obtained from Stan Kroenke's purchase of 30 percent of the Rams team. In addition, another $71 million included a $46 million payment to the NFL ($20 million up front and $1.7 million per year for fifteen years); $12.5 million to the Fox TV Network if ratings slipped after the Rams transfer from Los Angeles, which is the nation's second-largest TV market; and $13 million in the waived Rams' share of money from the League's sale of expansion team franchises. The relocation expenses were financed through PSL funds.

The number of PSLs sold was 49,400. They ranged in price from $250 to $4,500 plus tickets, and PSL owners are required to purchase season tickets ranging from $320 to $360. The request for over 70,000 PSLs far exceeded the seats allocated. More than 52,000 PSLs, 5,300 club seats, and 90 luxury boxes were sold to local fans and businesses. PSLs raised some $74 million for St. Louis, and without these funds the Rams' move would not have been possible.

The subsidies to get football back to St. Louis did not end with cash paid to the Rams or the PSLs. The new state-of-the-art home was paid for with public funds. The final cost of the Trans World Dome was $301 million—$202 million for stadium construction and $99 million for land, demolition, and various fees.

## The Kiel Center

The Kiel Center was the second new sports venue to open in the 1990s. At that time it was home to several St. Louis teams, including the Blues (hockey), the Ambush (soccer), the Stampede (arena football), and the Vipers (roller hockey). The publicly built, owned, and operated Kiel Auditorium was razed in 1992 for construction of the privately backed 18,500-seat Kiel Center.

**Kiel Opera House and Auditorium. Photograph by Irv Schankman et al., Dorrill Studio, 1958. MHS Photographs and Prints.**

The agreement for building the Kiel Center was obtained by then-mayor Vincent Schoemehl Jr. after a falling-out in the late 1980s with Anheuser-Busch, which had wanted to build a new complex just south of Busch Stadium. After the brewery pulled out, the mayor sought investors for a new downtown arena to avoid the possibility of a new venue being located in St. Louis County, which was also seeking to build such a facility. Schoemehl negotiated a deal with the St. Louis corporate leadership that led to Kiel Partners (later known as Clark Enterprises).

Financing for the Center was complex. The Partners put up $135 million from five sources. City-issued bonds, privately guaranteed by the Kiel Center Partners, provided $62.5 million; the Partners themselves invested $30 million; $36.9 million came from loans from banks guaranteed by the Partners; deposits on suits and club seating netted $3.8 million; and $1.8 million came from investment earnings. In addition, $34.5 million was put up by the City from two separate bond issues: $10 million for demolishing the old Kiel Auditorium and $24.5 million for construction of a parking garage. The $10 million bond issue is financed using about $1 million of City revenue previously used to run the Arena, and the $24 million issue with $1.8 million from earmarked venue parking revenues.

The Kiel Center also received some financial protection by a deed restriction on the City-owned venue, the Arena, that barred it from holding any event that charged an admission price. In addition, Kiel Partners had a non-compete agreement with the publicly owned Trans World Dome which gave Kiel the right of first refusal for any event that could be accommodated at the Center. The City's actual commitment to Kiel had gone, de facto, considerably beyond the $35 million for demolition and garage construction.

The City's contribution includes $10 million for demolition of Kiel Auditorium and $24.5 million for a parking garage; providing a lease to Kiel Center Partners for seventy years at $1 per year and, since the City retains ownership, removing any property tax liability for the Partners; tearing down the historic Children's Building to provide more Kiel parking; eliminating booking of any events at the Arena so as not to compete with Kiel, thus eliminating the City's main source of revenue to pay off the outstanding debt on the Arena; reducing construction costs by issuing bonds backed by City assets; and agreeing to tear down the City jail located across from Kiel.

Kiel's name was changed to the Savvis Center in 2000. It has been very well received by the community. It is a state-of-the-art venue that hosts a variety of sports events, concerts, and other activities. While having received private backing from the St. Louis corporate elite and substantial public support, other financial issues also had to be resolved.

As mentioned earlier, the owner of the Blues hockey team, which plays at Savvis, put the team and its lease up for sale in 2005. If the team were to leave town the Center's financial viability would be in question. The owner's original intent was to acquire a basketball team that also would play at Savvis. Basketball never materialized, and the Blues went on the auction block.

## Beer and Baseball: Busch Stadium

Originally the Cardinals played in "old" Busch Stadium, which was known as Sportsman's Park until bought by the brewery. "Gussie" Busch was then instrumental in getting the "new" Busch Stadium built downtown; it was completed in 1966. Busch Stadium was built as one element of a much larger development effort which would include a new downtown stadium to seat about 50,000 for both baseball and football. This would provide a new home for both Cardinals teams and also become an anchor for more extensive renewal efforts. The stadium proposal was received with great enthusiasm.

**Sportsman's Park during the 1948 All-Star Game.
Photograph, 1948. MHS Photographs and Prints.**

To undertake the actual redevelopment project the Civic Center Redevelopment Corporation (CCRC) was formed as owner-developer under Missouri's Urban Redevelopment Corporations Law. August Busch Jr. was on its board of directors and provided financial support. This board also comprised a virtual who's who of the 1960s St. Louis business elite.

The CCRC was operated under an unusual three-way agreement which also included the City and the Land Clearance for Redevelopment Authority (LCRA), which acted as the packager for land purchase and demolition using its eminent domain powers. CCRC contracted with LCRA for all land acquisition and clearance and the actual construction. Ownership was then transferred to CCRC. Public funding for this project was limited to $6 million for public improvements around the stadium. No other public funds were used for construction. The stadium was completed in 1966 at a cost of $26 million; with the four adjacent parking garages the total investment was $51 million.

In 1981 Anheuser-Busch purchased Busch Stadium from the CCRC for $53 million. When it was first built, the property taxes on the CCRC property were abated under a program aimed at stimulating development projects. The stadium initially made contributions in lieu of taxes beginning at about $150,000 in 1967. However, in 1993 the brewery paid full taxes exceeding $1 million per year. All things considered, the initial $6 million infrastructure investment by the City paid off. Minimal public support for a large-scale private venture led to expanded property and amusement tax receipts plus a focus for major urban redevelopment.

**Aerial view of Busch Stadium and the Gateway Arch, September 21, 1967. Photograph by Ted McCrea, 1967. MHS Photographs and Prints.**

In 1995 Anheuser-Busch announced its decision to sell the team. Prior to this, these plans had been kept a near-total secret. The brewery stated its intent to keep the Cardinals in St. Louis. Any deal for the Cardinals was to be a package that included the team, the stadium, parking garages, and adjacent land.

The new owners introduced themselves on December 22, 1995, and announced their purchase from the brewery for $150 million. The deal stipulated that the stadium would keep the Busch name for at least fifteen years. The investors were composed of local business representatives and also included William O. DeWitt Jr., whose family has been involved in baseball for about fifty years ("New Cards Owners" 1995).

It is obvious that the decision of Anheuser-Busch to package the team with the stadium and parking garages made the deal far more attractive for a local purchase. The efforts of local business interests to finance the purchase avoided loss of the team. This in turn eliminated the threat of St. Louis having to go into the market for a new baseball team with a thirty-year-old stadium.

The purchase of the Cardinals kept the team in town under mostly local ownership. However, this did not end the stadium issue. The new owners almost immediately began to push for a new publicly funded stadium to replace the thirty-five-year-old ballpark. There was talk of moving to a new venue in St. Louis County, and the State of Illinois expressed interest as well. In the end the new facility was built virtually exactly where the old stadium stood, with mostly private funds but some support from St. Louis City and County and the State of Missouri. It was slated to open in July 2006. The ballpark would be "partnered" with a mixed-use Ballpark Village that includes retail, entertainment, and residential facilities. The team has committed to supporting the Ballpark Village development at a total cost of nearly $700 million.

### From Cows to Hockey: The St. Louis Arena

The Arena came into existence as a "cow palace" at a cost of $2.3 million. It opened in 1929. Privately financed, it involved local beer baron August Busch Jr. and steel entrepreneur Henry Scullin. At the time it was a large facility with a seating capacity near 18,000.

**Aerial view of the Arena. Photograph by Ralph Rugh, 1930. MHS Photographs and Prints.**

The Arena's entry into sports was not until much later, in 1967, when Sidney Solomon Jr. bought it after being promised an NHL franchise. He spent $7 million on improvements, then brought in the Blues. They played their first game in October 1967 and continued to play there until moving to the Kiel Center in 1994. In 1977 Solomon sold the team and the Arena to the St. Louis–based Ralston Purina Company for about $13 million. Under this ownership, the Arena was renamed the Checkerdome, after its corporate logo. After reportedly losing millions of dollars on the team, Ralston tried to unload the hockey package by offering to sell the team to Civic Progress. It declined the offer, and the Blues nearly folded in 1983. Ralston finally sold both the team and the Checkerdome to an out-of-town investor, Harry Ornest, at a bargain-basement price. The Arena was $5 million plus an undisclosed amount for the team, probably on the order of $2–3 million. Soon after his purchase Ornest tried to move the team to Canada but failed. Three years later, in 1986, he sold the Blues and the Arena for over $30 million. At this point the Blues team and the Arena venue were split.

A Civic Progress–based group purchased the Blues team from Ornest for $19 million, and the City of St. Louis bought the Arena for $15 million from bond proceeds. This eliminated the constant threat of it being moved out of town by the first financially attractive deal. As long as the Blues played at the Arena they paid the City an annual rent of $1 million, which helped with the $1.7 million in annual interest on the bonds. Once they moved to the Kiel Center the rent stopped, but the City still had to pay off the outstanding Arena debt.

As a strange twist on public support, as a part of the Kiel Center deal the City was asked to not use the Arena for any event that might compete with Kiel nor charge an admission fee for any event. A deed restriction was placed on the Arena to this effect. Thus, the City owned a valuable piece of property in a prime location but with deed restrictions that precluded any revenue generation from its use. These restrictions would vanish if the Arena was torn down. It sat idle for thirteen years and was demolished finally in 1999 for commercial development.

Curiously, what had begun as a private development in the late 1920s eventually required public funds some sixty years later. The Blues were bought by a group of local investors, but the City then invested over $35 million to subsidize the construction of their new home, the Kiel Center. The City also assumed the ownership of the Arena at a cost of $15 million. The final public piece of the Arena/Blues financial puzzle was the deed restriction that precluded any revenue for the City. The Blues stayed in town, but almost $50 million in public funds were expended to accomplish this.

# Public Funds and Sports Venues in St. Louis

Even for those St. Louis sports venues that were "private" ventures, the public was involved with either cash or other types of concessions with financial implications. The menu of public involvement, past and present, is quite extensive. Table 2 summarizes project cost, who paid, public concessions,  and identifiable public receipts.

## Table 2. A Snapshot of St. Louis Sports Venue Assets

**Sportsman's Park**

**Date opened:** originally in 1872; expanded in 1902

**Project cost:** about $500,000

**Public funds:** none

**Public concessions:** none

**Public receipts:** normal taxes and fees

**St. Louis Arena**

**Date opened:** 1929; was demolished in 1999

**Project cost:** $2.3 million

**Public funds:** none; originally, it was developed as a private venture

bought for $15 million by the City with a bond issue

**Public concessions:** the City facilitated the Blues' purchase by buying the Arena

deed restriction placed on the Arena to not compete with the new Kiel Center and not charge admission

for any event

**Public receipts:** normal taxes, fees, and charges

about $1 million per year rent from the Blues (after it closed the rent stopped)

**Kiel Auditorium**

**Date opened:** 1934; torn down in 1992 to build the Kiel Center

**Project cost:** $6 million

**Public funds:** funded with proceeds from a City bond issue

**Public concessions:** operated as a municipal auditorium until torn down to build Kiel Center

**Public receipts:** derived from normal operations as a municipal facility

**Busch Stadium**

**Date opened:** 1966

**Project cost:** $51 million total: $26 million stadium, $25 million parking garages

**Public funds:** $6 million for project-related infrastructure from a City bond issue

**Public concessions:** developed using eminent domain powers for land acquisition and demolition

property tax relief over twenty-five years: for ten years tax is on land value only and the next fifteen years on land

value and 50 percent of the improvements' value

**Public receipts:** no funds specifically earmarked since a private facility

as of 1993 full property taxes in excess of $1 million per year

general tax receipts from venue operations

**Kiel Center**

**Date opened:** 1994

**Project cost:** $169.5 million

**Public funds:** $34.5 million total: $24.5 million garage, $10 million demolition of Kiel Auditorium

**Public concessions:** deed restriction on Arena to preclude its competition with Kiel

non-compete provision with Trans World Dome favoring Kiel

bonds issued by public authority with tax exempt status

City participation allowed the use of federal tax breaks

no property taxes since publicly owned

**Public receipts:** parking revenues

general tax receipts from venue operations

Table 2 (Cont'd). A Snapshot of St. Louis Sports Venue Assets

**Trans World Dome (now Edward Jones Dome)**

**Date opened:** 1995

**Project cost:** $301 million

**Public funds:** $296.8 million: $4.2 million from private PSL funds; 50 percent State; 25 percent County; 25 percent City (general revenue is used for State and City, hotel/motel tax for the County)

**Public concessions:** no property taxes, publicly owned

financed with tax exempt bonds

City eminent domain powers

**Public receipts:** $250,000 per year lease; no inflation adjustment

$1.5 million per year advertising

$325,000 per year from TWA, 3.5 percent annual inflation adjustment

general tax receipts from venue operations

**Busch Stadium**

**Date opened:** 2006

**Project cost:** $388 million

**Public funds:** $45 million loan from St. Louis County

$30.4 million in state tax credits for infrastructure and site work

$12.3 million from the Missouri Department of Transportation for Interstate 64 ramp relocation

$3.4 million/year from elimination of City's entertainment ticket tax

**Public concessions:** elimination of the entertainment ticket tax

**Public receipts:** all normal taxes and fees and charges

# Lessons from the St. Louis Experience

Several things stand out from a review of St. Louis's long-term involvement in its sports assets. First, use of public funds has been relatively recent, some $400 million in facility construction in the 1990s with another near $400 million in the 2000s. Public investment can escalate very quickly, especially given the competition for professional teams and their ability to extract significant public support. The new downtown economic strategy is tourism, amusement, and sports. The infrastructure to link into this new economic base can be very costly. Image and status played an important role in St. Louis's decisions about its sports assets, as did financial returns.

A second feature is that the public sector can become involved in more ways than just money. The City began with Busch Stadium by making a small expenditure for infrastructure but then granted property tax relief which amounted to millions of dollars over time. Eminent domain powers were also used for Busch to allow the redevelopment package to be assembled. By the time the Kiel Center deal was assembled, the City was in much deeper. Direct funds involved almost $35 million for construction. Another $15 million was spent to purchase the Arena. Packaging Kiel, a nominally private venture, required $50 million in outlays plus a variety of other concessions.

With the Trans World Dome the City investment made a quantum jump. It, de facto, assumed 25 percent of a $720 million commitment with a direct annual cost of $6 million. From this it initially got an identifiable $2 million from the lease and advertising fees. This leaves some $4 million that must come from general revenues from Dome events and Rams activities and indirectly from other economic activity. Curiously, the manner in which Dome financing was split might have been a good deal for the City. It has a downtown $300 million venue which, in addition to Rams games, can link the City to a higher rung of convention meeting business. It pays 25 percent, and the State of Missouri and St. Louis County pay 75 percent of the cost.

St. Louis has been involved in sports for more than a century. The numerous teams and venues and public support attest to the value the community places on these assets. They have contributed to the local economy, been focal in downtown urban restructuring, generated tax revenues, and last, but by no means least, given St. Louis an image as a sports town.

### References

Note: In addition to specific sources below, general background information was derived from various issues of the *St. Louis Post-Dispatch*. The *Information Please Sports Almanac* (Boston: Houghton Mifflin, various years) provided a wealth of data on teams, playing fields, and events.

Ahmed, Safir. "Escape from St. Louis." *The Riverfront Times*, January 24, 1996, pp. 18–21.

Civic Center Redevelopment Corporation. *First Annual Report*. St. Louis: Civic Center Redevelopment Corporation, 1963.

Coopers & Lybrand. *City of St. Louis: An Analysis of Net New Fiscal Benefit Generated from the Construction and Operation of the Expanded Cervantes Convention Center*. Report for the St. Louis NFL Corporation. Dallas: Coopers & Lybrand, February 27, 1991a.

———. *State of Missouri: An Analysis of Net New Fiscal Benefit Generated from the Construction and Operation of the Expanded Cervantes Convention Center*. Report for the State of Missouri. Dallas: Coopers & Lybrand, February 27, 1991b.

Development Strategies. *Economic and Tax Impacts: St. Louis Cardinals Proposed New Ballpark and Ballpark Village, Downtown St. Louis, Missouri.* St. Louis: Development Strategies, 2000.

East-West Gateway Coordinating Council. *Where We Stand: The Strategic Assessment of the St. Louis Region.* 4th ed. St. Louis: East-West Gateway Coordinating Council, 2002.

Hellinger, Daniel. "Finally Flim-Flam Football." *St. Louis Journalism Review* 25, no. 176 (May 1995a): 1.

————. "Most Reporters Were Uncritical Promoters of Stadium Financing." *St. Louis Journalism Review* 25, no. 177 (June 1995b): 1.

Industrial Development Authority of the City of St. Louis. "Preliminary Official Statement" for bond issue dated October 27, 1992, Prudential Securities Incorporated.

Korr, Charles. "Sports and Recreation." In *St. Louis Currents: Essays on St. Louis*, edited by FOCUS St. Louis, 162–172. St. Louis: FOCUS St. Louis, 1997.

Land Clearance for Redevelopment Authority. *Downtown Sports Stadium Project Redevelopment Plan, Revised Edition.* St. Louis: Author, July 20, 1965.

Laslo, David, Claude Louishomme, Donald Phares, and Dennis R. Judd. "Building the Infrastructure of Urban Tourism: The Case of St. Louis." In *The Infrastructure of Play: Building the Tourist City*, edited by Dennis R. Judd. New York: M. E. Sharpe, 2003.

Meserole, Mike, ed. *The 1996 Information Please Sports Almanac.* New York: Houghton Mifflin, 1995.

Miklasz, Bernie. Column, *St. Louis Post-Dispatch*, January 22, 1995, p. 1F.

Missouri Economic Research and Information Center. *Economic Impacts of the Proposed St. Louis Ballpark Stadium and Village.* Jefferson City, MO: Department of Economic Development, #LRS–0302–1, March 2002.

"New Cards Owners: 'We Want to Win.'" *St. Louis Post-Dispatch*, December 23, 1995.

Phares, Don. "Sports Under the Arch: St. Louis Teams, Venues, and Public Funds." Paper presented at Sport in the City: Cultural, Economic, and Political Considerations, University of Memphis, November 9–12, 1996.

Regional Commerce and Growth Association. *Annual Economic Impact of the NFL Rams on the St. Louis Region.* St. Louis: Author, 1996.

Rosentraub, Mark. *The Cardinals, A New Ballpark, and Major League Baseball: A Road Map for Success.* St. Louis: Public Policy Research Center, University of Missouri–St. Louis, 2000.

————, ed. "Cities, Sports, and Imagery." In *Major League Losers.* New York: Basic Books, 1999.

St. Louis Regional Convention and Sports Complex Authority. *1994 Annual Report.* St. Louis: Sports Complex Authority, 1995.

# Chapter 5

# Amateur Sports in St. Louis

**Sharon Smith**

One way a city gains recognition, and often prominence, is through sports. Sports teams automatically bring travelers to the city. Professional teams bring national publicity as the opposing teams come to town bringing their own fans, and the national spotlight shines even brighter if the home team advances to the play-offs and championships. But any one city can only afford to have so many professional sports teams, and it is beyond imagination to have more than one team in any single sport, save for league-straddling baseball and football. However, amateur sports are different. A city can boast many teams in the same sport, and these teams can, and often do, compete against each other. And single players might also emerge as an emissary for the sport and the city.

St. Louis is a city that knows the value of sports. One cannot talk about sports without looking at the various marks St. Louis has made on the sports world. But in order to fully appreciate what St. Louis has to offer today in both professional and amateur sports, one must go back to the roots of these sports.

# Variations on the Sport of Baseball

### The Khoury League

St. Louis has been, is, and always will be a great sports town. It has a very gloried past when it comes to baseball, for instance. However, the reference here is not to the Cardinals and the Browns, but rather to the other various baseball-like sports. St. Louis is the home of George and Dorothy Khoury, founders of the Khoury League. The Khourys wanted a place on the south side of St. Louis for their three boys, Al, Bob, and George Jr., to play baseball. In the summer of 1936, Dorothy organized a team, the Warriors. George, with the help of some friends, found an open lot at Spring and Chouteau to use as the ball field. While George was working to secure the lot, he learned of the number of boys who claimed they had nothing to do and no place to play. His original intent to provide a place for his sons to play evolved into the organization of an entire league.

He started with eight teams that began playing on Mother's Day, 1936. By 1947 the league had grown to include two thousand St. Louis–area boys playing Khoury League baseball. In 1965, 750,000 boys played in 3,000 Khoury Leagues in thirteen states and five countries that included the Dominican Republic, Canada, Panama, Japan (Okinawa), and Israel (Burnes 1965).

The managers organized their teams by age, the youngest team consisting of seven-year-old boys. They made the baseball diamonds smaller and scaled down the equipment to fit the boys, changing them as necessary. In the case of some teams, the boys grew up together. In 1954 Husmann and Roper Freight Lines, Inc., sponsored a Khoury League team of boys ranging in age from seven to nine years old. Known as the H and R Redheads, the boys entered the Junior Division in 1966 still together as a team. They had the best team in their division in six of their eight years together (Burnes 1965).

The Khoury League division of youth baseball is one of the oldest youth organizations in the United States. It is still active today, and each year the teams open their season on Mother's Day to honor Dorothy Khoury.

From the Khoury League grew the Little Leagues and the Pony Leagues, also designed for youth. Often these leagues develop teams that advance out of the city, going to state championships and possibly even the Little League World Series.

The St. Louis area has numerous Khoury Leagues, and Belleville has the largest and oldest Khoury League in Illinois. Along with the numerous youth baseball Khoury Leagues, St. Louis can also boast numerous Khoury-style softball leagues.

## Corkball

St. Louis is also the city that invented corkball, predominantly in the German neighborhoods around the local taverns. Legend suggests the game originated in an East St. Louis tavern in the early 1900s when a man began tossing bottle caps to another man who whacked at them with a broomstick. Bottle caps originally were lined with a cork that caused the cap to move rapidly when hit. Another legend says that corkball began in a brewery in Carondelet where brewery workers would pass their lunch breaks carving balls out of the cork bungs that plugged the holes in the beer barrels ("Local Game Makes Good" 1959). Corkball seems to be a sport of resourcefulness, and other objects were used before there were actual corkballs. Lew Grossgloss, retired vice president of Casey's Sporting Goods, recalls that his father would stuff BBs into a fishing cork and wrap the cork with tape (Corrigan 1979). The idea stuck, and since then corkball grew up and has grown into a major pastime in St. Louis.

By 1930 the first organized leagues began. Cages were used by teams as early as 1940 (Leech 2005). According to "Mr. Corkball," Don Young, cages became popular after World War II as a way to counteract kids' fascination with television. Young played for the South St. Louis Corkball League, founded in 1936 as the Grupp Corkball League (Corrigan 1979).

Corkball is great for neighborhood cohesion because it can be played by as few as two players to a side. Players of all ages can play since there is virtually no running in corkball, a feature that helps in the hot St. Louis summers. Ted Wagner of the *St. Louis Post-Dispatch* said he "played it from morning till late afternoon all summer long" (Wagner 1958).

A team usually consists of a pitcher, catcher, outfielder, and possibly second catcher. Charles Baker described a team like this: "You have a pitcher, catcher, and an umpire calling balls and strikes, and the rest of the guys drink beer" (Kelley 1991). It seems that beer drinking does go along with corkball in many leagues.

In corkball, the field can be the street or cages. The rules are certainly modified from those of the parent game, baseball. The pitcher is only fifty-five feet from the batter, five and a half feet closer than in baseball, and the game is fast pitch, thrown overhand from a mound. A batter is out if he swings and misses the ball and the catcher holds onto it. Two called strikes are an out, again only if the catcher holds onto the ball. A foul tip caught by the catcher is also an out. A fly ball caught by the pitcher or outfielder is an out. The batter cannot bunt. A hit means there is a "base runner," but the base runner exists only on paper. Every hit is a single, unless otherwise designated by the local field rules, and four hits count as a run. Then each subsequent hit counts as another run. A home-run marker is established, and anything hit past the marker is a home run, counting every "runner" on base as well. There are three outs in an inning, and five innings make up a game.

The equipment for corkball is a bit different from that of baseball as well. The ball is much smaller but looks very much like a baseball, down to the sewn leather cover. Markwort Sporting Goods of St. Louis, a major supplier of corkballs, began when Herb Markwort Jr. decided he could make little baseballs rather than continue wrapping the tape around the corks (Pierce 2000). The ball, however, got its name from the other type of homemade ball made by taking a round piece of cork purchased from the local dime store and wrapping it with tape. Sometimes the ball was loaded with shot as well for extra weight (Wagner 1958). The bats are also of two different varieties. The regulation bats are made by Spaulding or Louisville Slugger and resemble their baseball counterparts, except that the diameter is much smaller. In the homemade variety a broomstick is used, as in the original game.

Many corkball cages were located near taverns. Often the tavern sponsored the team, paying the initial fees for installing the cage, which back in 1950 varied from $500 to $800. At that time there were twenty-two enclosed corkball courts in St. Louis. While corkball cages are not seen much anymore, corkball is still played around the city in wide open spaces, in places like Jefferson Barracks corkball fields and Tower Grove corkball fields.

**Softball**
Softball is a sport for all people of all ages, but St. Louis women's softball is an important part of the fabric of sports in St. Louis. Girls and young women have participated in both slow-pitch and fast-pitch softball. Often the leagues compete for city titles. Team sponsors such as Kutis Funeral Home are involved every year. Going back to the 1970s, young women playing for teams like Kutis were considered the best in St. Louis. These women had other professions—often they were teachers and looked forward to playing ball in the summer. Out of this setting grew the Women's Professional Softball League (WPSL) in 1976. St. Louis formed a team, the St. Louis Hummers, in 1977. The Hummers were a good team fielded by players who had played for Kutis and other semiprofessional teams. The league folded in 1979, but for the three years the Hummers were in the league they made it to the playoffs.

From that history, St. Louis softball continues to encourage girls to play hard at the sport they love. There are practice batting cages and instructional areas to learn the art of the sport, and in one location ex-pro

Vicki Schneider offers instruction. Her goal, it seems, is to give girls the same opportunities she had to play softball.

The Metro St. Louis Amateur Softball Association (ASA) office is located on Page Avenue and is a local member of the ASA of America. According to the group's Web site, St. Louis will be the host for the 2006 Junior Olympic Girls 10U "B" Fast Pitch National Championship. Women's softball leagues are very active in the city, and it is possible that this will lead to the formation of another professional team.

## Baseball

No discussion of amateur sports in St. Louis would be complete without baseball. St. Louis has many amateur baseball teams, both adult and preparatory or select youth leagues. Amateur teams were formed as early as the 1850s and have continued to the present. Until the mid-1860s the St. Louis teams played only each other, but in 1867 the St. Louis Unions hosted the Washington, D.C., Nationals. The Nationals won that contest 113 to 26 (Leech 2005).

**St. Louis Ford Dealers infielder tagging an Eagle Motors Ford runner at third base during an unidentified baseball game.**
**Photograph, no date. MHS Photographs and Prints.**

Then there was Pope Sturgeon. "Sturgeon, according to the remembrance of old timers on the diamond here, used the form of delivery to send across the plate a whirling drop that effectively fooled batters long years before it was taken up in the big leagues" (Murray 1927). The pitch referred to here is the spitball. Sturgeon, at the age of nine, could throw a wicked curveball at a time when most professional pitchers were not yet aware of such a pitch. He was a star pitcher for school teams and amateur teams all his life, but he never went professional because he believed he couldn't earn enough. Despite this, he "presents a record of 106 contests won without a single defeat" (Murray 1927).

Hubert "Dickey" Ballentine and St. Louis City police captain Tom Brooks organized a baseball team in 1954 for the African American children in north St. Louis, giving them an opportunity to play a team sport. In 1956 Martin Mathews, a semiprofessional ballplayer, became manager of another north St. Louis neighborhood team. Ballentine and Mathews met one day at Hanley Park, where their two teams were practicing. They discussed the need to form a club for these children since there seemed to be a great demand for kids to play ball. Out of this discussion grew the Mathews-Dickey Boys' Club, begun in 1960. In 1961 the club's juvenile team won its division's championship in the Khoury League. Four years later there were thirty-seven baseball teams in the club. By 1975 the club grew to include seventy-five baseball teams as well as football and basketball teams. To this day, the Mathews-Dickey Boys' Club exists to give children a place to play organized sports along with many other amenities.

Hidden Assets

Left and above: Baseball players in the Pruitt-Igoe League with their
trophies at the ninth annual Mathews-Dickey Boys' Club benefit dinner.
Photograph by James Carrington, 1970. MHS Photographs and Prints.

There are many amateur teams in the St. Louis area that actively recruit young players. The St. Louis Aviators is a twelve-and-under select baseball team that plays between forty and fifty games a season with the possibility of several out-of-town tournaments. The St. Louis Rivermen is an eleven-and-under team; the Ballwin Athletic Association seeks players seven years old and younger. The Fenton Athletic Association accommodates players in the Atom 2 level of Khoury League through high school age. There is another team for under-eleven-year-olds who live in the Ritenour, Normandy, Berkeley, Ferguson, or Florissant school districts. A Midget 1 level Khoury team, the Classic Cars Titans, is for players twelve and under. They play at the Affton Athletic Association and hope for five to ten tournaments a year. A full listing of calls for youth teams can be found at www.stltoday.com under sports and the subcategory of "other sports."

# St. Louis Is a Soccer Town

If St. Louis is a baseball town, it most assuredly is also a soccer town. Many cities await the local rivalry between high school football teams, usually billed as the fall classic on Thanksgiving or New Year's Day. "In St. Louis our big game is an extension of our history. For more than a century, rivalries between schools, neighborhoods, and ethnic groups have been played out on the soccer field" (Lipsitz 1983). It is an ethnic sport derived from the European working class. "German brewery workers, Italian terra-cotta craftsmen, Scottish railroad employees (Blue Bells) and Irish factory hands had little in common beyond the alienations of labor, but soccer provided a common activity" (Lipsitz 1983). Working-class neighborhoods in St. Louis also could find their identity on the soccer fields. The Kensingtons, named for the street on the north side where most of the players lived, proved themselves one season: In 1889–1890 the team won every game without giving up a goal to their opposition, "a circumstance interpreted as clear proof of the superiority of that street to the rest of the city by its inhabitants" (Lipsitz 1983).

Organized soccer in St. Louis dates back to November 24, 1881, when the first game was recorded between the Athletic Club and Mound City. The Athletic Club won 1–0. The *St. Louis Globe-Democrat* reported on January 30, 1882, that one thousand fans saw a soccer game between the

Hornets and Mike Walsh's Eleven played at Sportsman's Park (Rodriguez 1980). Many of the early soccer clubs were affiliated with churches and, later, manufacturing and retail companies, unlike other communities where soccer seemed to flourish around ethnic clubs. "Factories like Scullin Steel and St. Louis Screw sponsored soccer teams to provide recreation and a chance to vent the frustrations of the work week for their employees" (Lipsitz 1983). One writer suggests that Catholic parishes adopted soccer "as an inexpensive mass participation sport for their recreational programs, and it wasn't long before the top teams were winning national honors. One result of this is the long history in St. Louis of developing home grown talent rather than attracting foreign players to the top level professional leagues" (Litterer 2005).

Early on, St. Louis was considered the western outpost for soccer. St. Louis was known for its amateur clubs, which won national championships such as the U.S. Open Cup and National Amateur Cup in the 1950s. In the years between 1920 and 1957, six different St. Louis teams won the U.S. Open Cup. The first soccer dynasty in St. Louis was St. Leo's Parish, made up of players from around Twenty-fifth Street and Mullanphy. They played at Kingshighway and Easton, known then as the old CBC field, and at Clayton and Tamm, the West End Soccer League field (Litterer 2005, Lipsitz 1983). They won nine consecutive championships from 1905 to 1913. The team even toured the east, playing a series in New Jersey. By 1915 the amateur St. Louis Municipal League had formed, and the Ben Millers began to dominate. They won three consecutive league championships from 1915 to 1918. The league had thirty different teams representing various neighborhoods, churches, and businesses. The league used fields in parks across the city, including Carondelet, O'Fallon, Fairgrounds, and Forest Park.

The league was eligible for U.S. Open Cup play once they joined with the U.S. Soccer Federation (USSF). The Ben Millers, representing St. Louis, made it to the U.S. Open Cup and won in 1920. The Ben Millers team was composed entirely of St. Louisans, while the second-place team, Fore River Shipyard from Quincy, Massachusetts, used eleven players of British descent. The St. Louis team the Scullin Steels followed in the St. Louis tradition, going to the U.S. Open Cup in 1921, winning it in 1922, and sharing co-champion status in 1923. As Litterer (2005) points out, industry-sponsored teams often were short lived if "team performance did not mesh with corporate bottom lines. . . . Sometimes they were dropped when the profit margin fell, regardless of team performance."

St. Louis may well have been the soccer capital of the world in the 1930s and 1940s, according to Geoffrey Douglas, author of *The Game of Their Lives* (2005). He says of St. Louis: "A million fans a year attended hundreds of matches in at least a dozen parks and fields. The rivalries were ethnic and religious—the Germans, the Spanish, the Irish of Kerry Patch, the Italians of Little Italy and Dago Hill—the sons of urban Catholic immigrants . . . slugging out their hatreds and escaping their trials in ninety-minute, mostly bloodless wars" (Douglas 2005, 26). Immigration limits in the 1920s and the movement of the working class to the suburbs in the 1950s changed the look and tradition of soccer from the early days. The St. Louis Municipal League had 49 teams in 1943 and 119 teams by 1947, but the league had disbanded by 1957 (Lipsitz 1983; Rodriguez 1980). Khoury League soccer sponsored by businesses such as Kutis began in the mid-1950s, eventually replacing the former Municipal League (Litterer 2005).

When the amateur circuit faded, St. Louis again enjoyed the spotlight with Saint Louis University. The university added soccer to its list of varsity sports in 1959. The team posted NCAA national championships in 1959, 1960, 1962, 1963, and 1965, becoming another dynasty out of St. Louis. Soccer great Harry Keough became coach in 1967 and took the team to the championship the same year, where they played to a 0–0 draw and were named co-champions. Keough led them to NCAA titles in 1969, 1970, 1972, and 1973.

Since 1950 almost every World Cup team has had a St. Louis player on it. St. Louis continues to be a great soccer town. All one has to do is look around any field on a weekend to see soccer games abounding all around the metro St. Louis area.

# Dwight Davis and Tennis

St. Louis has a rich tennis history. Dwight Davis was born in St. Louis in 1879. He played in the 1904 Olympics in St. Louis and later was named St. Louis parks commissioner in 1911. During his time as commissioner he built many free tennis courts in the city. He is, of course, founder of the Davis Cup, the largest annual international team competition in the sport of tennis.

In the mid-1930s tennis great Earl Buchholz Sr. planned to go to California to teach tennis. A friend told him he'd get lost out there because

Action during a soccer game between Saint Louis University and Washington University at Musial Field. Photograph by James Carrington, 1969. MHS Photographs and Prints.

there were already too many tennis teachers. "What you should do is go to one of the worst tennis towns in the country, some place like St. Louis for instance" (Althoff 1960). Buchholz took the advice, and by 1960 St. Louis had become one of the top tennis towns in the United States. Seven of Buchholz's pupils won over twenty national championships between 1955 and 1960. Of the ten St. Louisans who had national ranking in 1960, six were his pupils (Althoff 1960).

The Triple A Golf and Tennis Club was established in 1897 and moved to Forest Park in 1902. It was a private club on public property until the early 1960s, when it opened to the public. It is the only local tennis center with clay courts. In 1966 the Triple A Golf and Tennis Club developed the Triple A Youth Foundation. Here St. Louis youth can learn the sports of tennis and golf. St. Louis is also home to the St. Louis District Tennis Association, a division of the Missouri Valley Section of the U.S. Tennis Association. And St. Louis can also boast of the Dwight Davis Tennis Center, located in Forest Park, which is open to all ages and skill levels. Tower Grove Park has three grass courts for public use, along with twelve hard courts. Grass courts are rare, and players who use those in Tower Grove may not get another opportunity to play on grass until they proceed to championships.

# Cycling in St. Louis

Some people would say that St. Louis is a bicycling town. The bicycle first appeared on St. Louis streets in 1878. Johnny Blow, agent for the Columbia Bicycle firm, brought the bicycle to the city to show it off and give riding lessons. People gathered from all around to view this latest spectacle. Blow also organized the St. Louis Bicycle Club in hopes of selling more bicycles.

Another organization, the St. Louis Cycling Club, the oldest cycling club in the nation, formed in 1887 "when the high wheeler, better known as the 'ordinary,' was still the standard model and only those possessed of a rare and foolhardy brand of courage would even dream of riding one" (Terry 1953). These early bicycles had one very large front wheel and a very small back wheel. The theory was that the larger the front wheel, the faster the cycle would go. Some front wheels were as large as sixty-four inches with a back wheel as small as twelve inches. Cycling with these vehicles was actually quite dangerous. A small pebble could throw the rider, and, given the size of the wheel, it was a long way down. It is no wonder then that cyclists were among the proponents of better roads. The Cycling Club also worked on a traffic light system. Before the bicycle, the horse had sole possession of the streets, but when cyclists became a part of the traffic flow, there arose a need for order.

"By 1897, bicycles had become so thick in St. Louis they got to be a menace. . . . Young bloods were 'scorching' at fifteen and twenty miles an hour, and there were numerous accidents. A city ordinance was passed putting a speed limit of eight miles an hour on bikes inside the city limits" (Terry 1953). Around this time the safety bicycle came into vogue, first with rubber wheels, later with pneumatic tires. With the pneumatic tires, bicycling really began to grow in popularity. Cyclists used to ride on several stretches: Kingshighway, Lindell Boulevard, and Manchester Road from Grand Avenue out to Manchester.

This was also a sport in which women could take part. However, that decision was not met without its share of distaste in St. Louis as well as across the country: "Editors were shocked and wrote editorials. Ministers were outraged and said so from the pulpit. Doctors were worried and said it wasn't natural or healthful for a woman to ride a bike. But there was no stemming the tide. First they rode in split skirts. Then came the bloomer" (Terry 1953).

**Maud Dunning Hurck and an unidentified male companion crossing a bridge over the Meramec River on bicycles at Fenton, Missouri. Photograph, 1879. MHS Photographs and Prints.**

Many cycling clubs began to fade away with the advent of the automobile, but not the St. Louis Cycling Club. There was less publicity about bikers and their races, but nevertheless, they continued.

H. G. Wells, writing in the 1890s, predicted that the bicycle would be used in warfare. The St. Louis Cycling Club tried to make his prediction reality during World War I. The government considered adding a bicycle corps to the army. Jefferson Barracks contacted the club for assistance. Twenty-five members arrived at the Barracks armed with carbines. They were asked to inspect the tunnels at Meramec Park and report back. They carried out several other similar missions. As may be expected, cycling took an upswing during the Depression. After the Depression new bike styles were introduced, and the newest fashion was the English bicycle.

The St. Louis Cycling Club has always kept its membership at one hundred, even though there is a waiting list. Each prospective member must come with recommendations from two current members and must agree to submit to an investigation that might include home and family visits by current members.

**St. Louis Cycling Club members gathered around a monument erected by the club to fellow bicyclist William M. Butler. Photograph, ca. 1923. MHS Photographs and Prints.**

The Club is known for having sent ten members to various Olympics. Waldon Martin and Carl Schuette competed in Stockholm in 1912. Schuette placed third in the long distance race and was the only St. Louis member to ever place at the Olympics. Jim Freeman went to Antwerp in 1920, and John Boulicault went to Paris in 1924. Chester Nelsen Sr., an important St. Louis name in cycling, went to Amsterdam in 1928. He went to the Olympics again in London in 1948, this time as the coach for the U.S. Cycling Team, for which his son, Chester Jr., rode. "The Nelsens are not only the first family in cycling in St. Louis, but also in the entire United States. They hold the rare distinction of being the only family in the country which has ever placed three generations on a U.S. Olympic team in the same sport" (Althoff 1966). Don Nelsen competed in the 1964 Games in Tokyo.

There are numerous bicycle clubs in the St. Louis area. Cyclists ride for exercise, recreation, and causes such as the MS 150. The St. Louis Cycling Club meets on the fourth Wednesday of each month at SM Wilson Training Center, 2149 Hampton Avenue. Today the club focuses more on competitive riding, as opposed to its early incarnation as more of a touring club.

# St. Louis Community Games: Cricket, Hurling, and Bocce Ball

St. Louis is known for its distinctive communities, many of them ethnic in nature. Many of the amateur sports played in the neighborhoods reflect the culture of the people who live there. Cricket is a game that originated in England, based loosely on the game of baseball—there is, at least, a ball and bat involved. "The average Englishman . . . has not been able to understand how an American can waste these implements on his national pastime of baseball when he could put them to much better use playing the British national pastime of cricket. The average American regards cricket with puzzlement and wonders why the Englishman doesn't uproot his preposterous wickets, exchange his paddle-shaped bat for a Louisville Slugger, install a home plate and three bases and start treating the umpires with proper disrespect" (*St. Louis Globe-Democrat* 1960).

In the game of cricket there are eleven players to a team. The ball is about the same size as a baseball, but covered in red leather. The bat looks more like a paddle, about four and one-half inches on the flat, hitting side. The field is spacious, much like a baseball field, but the dominant feature in the center of the field is two wickets, twenty-two yards apart, facing each other. A wicket is made up of three round sticks, stuck into the ground, close enough so that a ball cannot go between them. These three sticks have a channel carved into the top of them and another two sticks, four inches round, are laid in the channel. These two sticks are called "bails," and a major part of the game involves having the ball hit the stumps and knock off the bails. The batsman is actually the player defending the wicket. If the bail falls, the batsman is out, similar to a strikeout in baseball.

The St. Louis Kutis Cricket Club, founded in 1958 by Bill Tatlock, was the oldest club in the Midwest Conference. The club was influential in 1963, bringing the sport to St. Louis as it re-established the Canada-U.S. cricket rivalry. Four teams played in St. Louis through the 1980s; the prominent club then was the Forest Park Cricket Club. The Forest Park club combined with the St. Louis Kutis club in 1987, and since then the Kutis teams have dominated the sport in St. Louis. The team won the Midwest Cricket League Championship in 1999, after fourteen years without a play-off appearance. Over the years the ethnic composition of cricket has evolved, and the current Kutis team is made up predominantly of players from Pakistan and India. On their Web site they state that they would like to attract more players from Pakistan, India, England, Sri Lanka, Australia, and the West Indies, keeping up their international tradition (www.midwestcricket.org).

If cricket isn't confusing enough, the Irish have brought the sport of hurling to St. Louis. Hurling is the national sport of Ireland and is growing in popularity in the United States. "Even though it predates soccer, rugby, field hockey, lacrosse and baseball, hurling combines skills from all of them" (Billhartz 2005). The equipment is similar to many of these sports. There is a ball that looks much like a baseball, with a cork interior and outward stitching called a sliothar (sounds like "bitter"). It is hit with a paddle that looks like an enlarged hockey stick made of ash wood, called a hurley. There is a goalpost on either end of the field. The object of the game is to put the sliothar through the goalpost: If it goes through the top the score is three points, if it goes through the bottom it is one point. There are two halves to a game, each consisting of thirty minutes. A team is made up of fifteen players including a goalkeeper, three fullbacks, three halfbacks, two midfielders, three half-forwards, and three full-forwards. "It's arguably one of the fastest field sports in the world with players moving the ball down the 150-meter pitch by either kicking it, swatting it with their hands or batting, balancing and bouncing it with the end of their hurleys" (Billhartz 2005). Hurling "evolved as a method of training Irish warriors for battle or in lieu of battle to settle disputes over property claims" (St. Louis Hurling Club 2005).

In the summer of 2002 Dan Lapke, Paul Rohde, and Patrick O'Connor founded the St. Louis Hurling Club on the south side of Tower Grove Park. The three former Milwaukee Hurling Club players wanted to bring the sport to the St. Louis area. By the autumn enough players had joined to hold scrimmages in Tower Grove. In March of 2003 hurlers appeared in the downtown and Dogtown St. Patrick's Day parades, introducing the sport to many St. Louisans. In September 2003 the St. Louis Hurling Club opened its first season with three teams: Brown & Brown Financial, Black Thorn Pub Sons of Liberty, and McGurk's Black Shamrocks. The Black Shamrocks won the first Gateway Cup. Restaurant Llewelyn's team, the Red Dragons, entered the league in 2004.

In its third year, the club had four teams and eighty members. The games are played on Saturday afternoons at the Parkway Northeast Middle School, and practices are held Wednesday evenings in Tower Grove Park. There is a spring and fall season. The St. Louis players range in age from eighteen to forty-four and include three women. They also sponsor a kids' clinic to teach the art of hurling to the younger crowd. The club is always looking for new members and will train players.

Finally, there is the sport of bocce ball, found predominantly among the Italian population, most notably on the Hill in St. Louis. Bocce ball seems relatively simple in comparison to those just mentioned. Bocce ball is a type of lawn bowling. In fact, it is one of the oldest lawn games, dating back to Egypt, 5000 BC.

Bocce ball is played with just two players or between two teams with as many as four players to a team. It can be played on many different surfaces, including courts, sand, or lawn. An official court is seventy-six feet long and twelve feet wide. The bocce balls, or *boccia*, are wooden and are four and one-fifth inches in diameter. There are eight balls to a set, four of one color and four of another. There is also a smaller ball, called the pallino. Once the pallino is rolled to its stopping point, the object of the game is to roll the bocce balls closest to the pallino. For each ball that one team rolls closest to the pallino, a point is scored. The game ends when a team reaches twenty points.

# Amateur Boxing around St. Louis

Often a person or a group of persons is responsible for bringing a sport to the city and making both the sport and the city popular. Both are true for boxing. Gus Holt, Hermann Kempf, Ed Boehm, Joe Kern, and Frank Doran met and created the South Broadway Athletic Club. It was incorporated in 1904. The club's first home was 611 Geyer Avenue. It later moved to Seventh and Shenandoah in 1914, and moved again in 1923 to its present location, 2301 South Seventh Street.

The *Globe-Democrat* started the local Golden Gloves Tournament in 1935, and South Broadway entered. In the years between 1942 and 1949, South Broadway's teams won the Golden Gloves every year except 1943, when they lost to the Buder Center team by one point. After the 1965 season, boxing seemed to fade away for twenty-eight years. However, in 1992 South Broadway bought the old Stag Athletic Club building at 3337 South Seventh Street, opened a new gym, and revived amateur boxing again.

Myrl Taylor is known as the father of St. Louis amateur boxing. The following tribute to Myrl appeared in one of his many obituaries: "Myrl Taylor personifies amateur boxing. A native of St. Louis, Myrl devoted a large portion of his life to advancing the sport in his home community and across the nation. In testament to his leadership, St. Louis became known as the best amateur boxing city in the United States" (USA Boxing 2004).

Myrl's father, Earl Taylor Sr., was a professional boxer. Inspired by his father, Myrl entered the Golden Gloves Tournament in 1948. Taylor fought 156 amateur bouts and won 145 of them. He began working outside of the ring in 1975 to bring the sport back to popularity.

In 1970, John Childress decided to become involved in changing the look of amateur boxing. He and his business partner and friend, John Clarkson, purchased a boxing team, the St. Louis Saints, in the amateur International Boxing League (IBL). Team boxing and the IBL were new concepts begun by national sports commentator Jack Drees; initially they were not met with much fervor from the fans. The audience wanted to see individuals playing the sport, rugged and hard, as always. Said Childress of the team concept, "This looked like it could be a great opportunity to get a lot of kids who didn't have anything else to do off the streets" (Posen 1970). Childress also spoke of the difference between amateur and professional boxing: "Amateur boxing in many ways is considerably more exciting than pro boxing. An amateur boxer has only three rounds to do his thing" (Posen 1970).

St. Louis was definitely shining at the 1976 Olympics when Spinks brothers Leon and Michael won gold medals in their respective classes.

Dan Kirner, alderman of the Twenty-fifth Ward and former boxer, was inducted into the local Boxing Hall of Fame sponsored by the Gateway Classic Foundation in 2002. Kirner said, "The primary purpose of amateur boxing is to keep kids out of trouble. It should keep them on the straight-and-narrow and help them learn respect. . . . It cuts down on crime" (Crone 2002).

Amateur boxing continues on some level in St. Louis. In 2005 at least four boxers represented St. Louis at the National Golden Gloves Tournament of Champions. Barry Dennis, Carlos Small, DeAndre Latimore, and Ken Scalbrough made it to the quarterfinals. Dennis took the decision in the championship round in his weight class by defeating 2005 U.S. Championships light flyweight bronze medalist Teddy Padilla 4–1. This was Dennis's first national title. Boxing matches can be seen at the St. Charles Family Arena or in someone's backyard. While not as widespread as some of the other sports, boxing is still alive in St. Louis.

# Conclusion

There are many other sports that could be listed among the amateur ranks in St. Louis. What about washers, croquet, handball, bowling, and football, among others? From school- and community-sponsored sports to sandlots, St. Louis is truly a sports town with some very strong ties to many sports, and some of those sports have made St. Louis a town to reckon with.

George Khoury had this to say about sportsmanship: "Sportsmanship is that quality of honorable behavior which, because of its courtesy, dignity, respect, cooperation, and trustworthiness, habitually wins the esteem of one's fellow person whether he be opponent or ally. Flashes of sportsmanship come to all of us, but real possession only comes to those who consistently hold the respect and loyalty of the community. For them, there are no alibis, no unnecessary abusive remarks, no scheming to win at any cost; but a genuine love of fair play, which makes them modest winners and gracious losers" (Khoury 2005).

St. Louis's sports enthusiasm is most reflected the variety of amateur sports played across neighborhoods. New teams form constantly, some in the more traditional sports of baseball and softball, and others in the less conventional games like cricket and hurling. There is enough enthusiasm and energy in St. Louis to make a success of any sport.

Rivalries will always exist between schools and neighborhoods—that is the constant. The variable is which sports will thrive and which will fade into history, replaced by the intrigue of learning a new game for a new day. That is the beauty of amateur sports. They change with the fabric of the society and culture in ways that professional sports are not able to do. From washers to corkball, St. Louis has made a name for itself in amateur sports. What will be the next St. Louis sport? Only time will tell, but we can be sure something will emerge.

**References**

Althoff, Shirley. "The Great Bike Race." *St. Louis Globe-Democrat*, August 7, 1966.

———. "He Made St. Louis a Top Tennis Town." *St. Louis Globe-Democrat*, July 24, 1960.

Billhartz, Cynthia. "St. Louisans Make Like the Irish and Start Hurling." *St. Louis Post-Dispatch*, August 22, 2005.

Burnes, Bob. "A Little Man with a Big Idea." *St. Louis Globe-Democrat*, August 1, 1965.

Corrigan, Don. "Cage Corkball." *St. Louis Magazine*, August 1979.

Crone, Thomas. "A Politician with Punch." *The Commonspace*, April 2002. http://www.thecommonspace.org/2002/04/churchstate.php.

Douglas, Geoffrey. *The Game of Their Lives.* New York: Harper Paperbacks, 2005.

East County Corkball League. "The History of Corkball." http://jroth34202.tripod.com/id2.html (accessed October 24, 2005).

Fister, Jeffrey. "Triple A Club Plans Improvements on Forest Park Facilities." *West End Word*, March 22, 1990.

Kelley, Tim. "Corkball, Clowning Around, Suit MAC's Baker." *Cherry Diamond* 85, no. 9 (October 1991).

Khoury, George. "Garner Area Youth Sports League Home Page." http://eteamz.active.com/gaysl/ (accessed October 25, 2005).

Ladder Golf. "Bocce Ball." http://www.laddergolf.com/bocce-ball.php (accessed October 25, 2005).

Leech, Richard. "The Evolution of Baseball in St. Louis." http://members.tripod.com/TheSportsCardBroker/BBStLouis.htm (accessed October 25, 2005).

Lipsitz, George. "Soccer and a Century of Solidarity." *St. Louis Magazine*, November 1983.

Litterer, Dave. "History of Soccer in St. Louis." http://www.sover.net/~spectrum/saintlouis.html (updated February 8, 2005).

———. "St. Louis Soccer League 1907–1939." http://www.sover.net/~spectrum/slsl.html (updated August 28, 2002).

"Local Game Makes Good." *Union Electric Magazine*, Summer, 1959.

Murray, Chris. "Pope Sturgeon—The Man Who Invented the Spitball." *St. Louis Globe-Democrat*, April 3, 1927.

Pierce, Charles P. "The Sport That Time Forgot." *Esquire*, June 2000.

Posen, Bob. "Childress: New Boxing Breed." *St. Louis Post-Dispatch*, February 15, 1970.

Rodriguez, Mary Louise. "An Historical Account of the Game of Soccer in the St. Louis Metropolitan Area." Paper, Southern Illinois University at Edwardsville, July 1980.

Sanford, Frank. "A Team That Grew Up." *St. Louis Globe-Democrat*, July 9, 1961.

South Broadway Athletic Club. "South Broadway Athletic Club Home Page." http://www.southbroadwayac.org (accessed October 25, 2005).

*St. Louis Globe-Democrat*. "The Wicket Game of Cricket," October 2, 1960.

St. Louis Hurling Club. "Club History." http://www.stlhurling.com (accessed October 25, 2005).

Terry, Dickson. "And the Wheels Keep Rolling Along." *St. Louis Post-Dispatch*, August 30, 1953.

USA Boxing. "2004 News and Notes: St. Louis and USA Boxing Lose Myrl Taylor." September 2, 2004. http://www.usaboxing.org (accessed October 25, 2005).

Waeckerle, Herb. "Corkballers Uncork New Craze." *St. Louis Globe-Democrat*, August 20, 1950.

Wagner, Ted. "You Had to 'Belong' in Those Days." *St. Louis Post-Dispatch*, March 16, 1958.

Woo, William. "Nice Try, Jolly Bad Luck at Cricket." *Kansas City Times*, August 28, 1961.

# Chapter 6

# The St. Louis Blues Scene

**Andrew Scavotto**

Hometown pride is powerful, and when I walk into BB's Jazz, Blues and Soups, I get a feeling that I can experience only in St. Louis. Part nightclub, part museum, the club's walls are covered with artifacts, vintage posters, and photographs. All of the artwork and memorabilia feature St. Louis artists, and as I listen to Bennie Smith and the Urban Blues Express, the music and surroundings combine to create a palpable sense of an authentic, deeply rooted St. Louis tradition.

It's Saturday night, and local treasure Bennie Smith sits at the front of the stage, playing trademark licks on his Stratocaster guitar. Bennie has played with legends such as Albert King, B. B. King, Aretha Franklin, and Ike Turner, but tonight most of his listeners probably don't realize that they're watching a living link to blues, rock n' roll and R&B history. Underappreciated but undeterred, he delivers a standout performance: The band draws people to the dance floor, and people of all ages and backgrounds enjoy the music.

Bennie's show provided the perfect ending to an eye-opening week of blues exploration, which started on Tuesday at Beale on Broadway with Kim Massie and the Solid Senders. Massie is a world-class singer with a deep, gospel-inspired voice, who draws constant comparisons to Etta James. On Wednesday I was back at BB's, checking out guitarist Alvin Jett and his band, Phat noiZ. Jett came up listening to rock guitarists such as Santana and Jimi Hendrix in addition to the blues greats, and his diversity of influence is evident when he tears through an inspired version of Hendrix's "Little Wing." On Thursday night, I stopped in at Hammerstone's to catch a set from Rondo's Blues Deluxe, and then I was off to see the Rich McDonough Blues Band, which never disappoints. McDonough's dominance of his instrument is remarkable—at one moment he's attacking his guitar with incredible speed and ferocity, and at another he's making it cry, playing softly before building toward another crescendo. He's accompanied by singer/harmonica and guitar player Les Moore, whose showmanship and vocal ability provide the perfect complement to McDonough's quiet, guitar-hero persona.

On Friday night, I started with Leroy Pierson's early set of country-flavored blues at BB's. Leroy is a historian, a musicologist, and a phenomenal storyteller, and when he finished I resisted the temptation to sit next to him at the bar. Instead I headed over to the Great Grizzly Bear in Soulard to check out the Soulard Blues Band. Founded in 1978 by bassist Art Dwyer, the band has become an institution, and its lineup has featured a who's who of St. Louis's top blues musicians. I closed the evening with Billy Peek at BB's. Peek began playing the blues in St. Louis in the 1950s, and he adds an appealing element of old-time rock n' roll to the local scene. During the 1960s, he toured the world playing guitar for Chuck Berry, and Peek still plays "Johnny B. Goode" and "Maybelline" better than anybody (including Chuck).

My amazing week of music sounds like an extravagant, carefully planned vacation, but I didn't travel more than ten minutes at any time, and the whole experience cost me only about $35 in cover charges. I had no trouble finding great music on a nightly basis, and my adventure illustrates something unique about the local culture: The City of St. Louis boasts a rich tradition that still thrives, and on any night in St. Louis one can enjoy easy, affordable access to some of the world's best blues.

Blues is a folk art rooted in African musical traditions. Brought to this country by slaves, the music is characterized by simple, repetitive rhythms and patterns. This basic form creates a trademark foundation for solos and improvisation, and in the words of local guitar legend Tom Maloney, "to be able to innovate within a form without losing the form is true artistic achievement." In America, the blues emerged as an expressive outlet for the pain caused by poverty, loneliness, and other hardships experienced by its creators. The blues originated as an artistic response to oppressive times, created not for commercial purposes, but to provide heartfelt expressions of the human experience. Rooted in harsh reality, the music comes from the soul. It's played with feeling, and the expression is genuine. According to St. Louis blues hero Henry Townsend, the blues are a way of communicating truth, and "if you lived it, you lived it—making it pretty don't help a bit" (Townsend 1999).

The local blues culture has roots traceable to the late 1800s and early 1900s. In his autobiography, W. C. Handy, known to some as "the Father of the Blues," describes traveling to St. Louis in 1892 and hearing guitar players on the Mississippi River levee playing a tune that began, "I walked all the way from East St. Louis / and I didn't have one po' measly dime." The song had numerous one-line verses that the musicians sang throughout the night, and Handy called the song "East St. Louis Blues" (Palmer 1982). Similarly, vaudeville legend Ma Rainey said she first heard the blues during her travels to Missouri in 1902, where she heard a girl singing a "strange" song about how her man had left her (Palmer 1982).

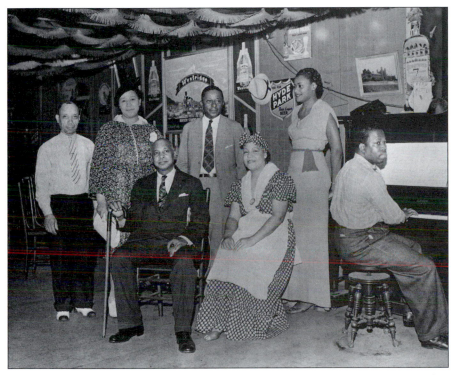

**W. C. Handy (seated with cane) visiting Old Rock House Saloon. Photograph by *St. Louis Globe-Democrat* staff, ca. 1935. MHS Photographs and Prints.**

This type of music could be heard coming out of the "sportin'" or "good time houses" located on or near the Mississippi River levee during the early 1900s, and several St. Louis artists also claim that the levee was known nationwide for the origination of the blues (Oliver 1965). Sporting houses on the levee attracted a rough crowd, and riverboats would often stop at the dock so that travelers could enjoy the whiskey, gambling, and music that characterized the area. Anecdotes from and interviews with artists from the early 1900s also identify neighborhoods filled with nightlife on Market Street, which featured the Rosebud Café, Morgan Street, and Third Street in East St. Louis as focal points in the early blues scene (Oliver 1965).

The river levee was a breeding ground for the blues, but during the early 1900s St. Louis was known primarily for its ragtime, a piano-based art form characterized by syncopated melodies and a "ragged," unrefined style. Ragtime provided a welcome contrast to the more rigid classical music of the time (think Sousa and Strauss), and Missouri was home to the genre's most legendary figures, such as Tom Turpin, Charles Thompson, and Scott Joplin. Joplin, known as "the King of Ragtime," traveled from Sedalia to St. Louis frequently, playing tunes such as the "Maple Leaf Rag" in piano parlors throughout the state. The area became a major ragtime center, and since St. Louis also hosted a booming publishing industry, the popularity of ragtime was enhanced by the easy availability of sheet music, which was pressed cheaply and distributed widely throughout the area. The music spread rapidly into people's parlors, and family entertainment often involved gathering around the piano to sing the popular rags.

The sheet music didn't show color, and the prevalence of ragtime allowed black music to gain widespread exposure in white communities. During the early 1900s, ragtime became so important that every bar and parlor in St. Louis featured a piano. Slower ragtime sounds a lot like the blues, and certain rags known as "slow drags" illustrate the similarities between the two art forms. Ragtime didn't necessarily precede the blues, but it helped lay the foundation for its acceptance. Ragtime contributed to the vitality of music in the city, St. Louis became known for its music scene, and out of this environment the blues emerged as a popular art form.

Along with the popularity of ragtime and the prevalence of nightlife and entertainment districts, most historians identify the city's central location and proximity to the Mississippi River as critical factors in the development of the blues in St. Louis. Typically blues is explained as a phenomenon that started in the southern delta and made its way up the Mississippi River as blacks migrated out of the South following the Civil War. Although the Mississippi River allowed many African Americans to migrate to St. Louis, historians note that the river was not the only factor

Scott Joplin. Halftone, 1904. MHS Library.

that led musicians to the area. Union Station made the city a huge railroad center, attracting many travelers who were going east and west, in addition to north and south. In fact, stowing away and "hoboing" on a railcar was most likely a lot easier than jumping on a riverboat (especially if you were carrying a guitar). Highways 49 and 61 came through St. Louis, and the city is centrally located between two other cities with rich musical traditions, Memphis and Chicago.

The Union Station train shed and station seen from Eighteenth Street. Photograph by Emil Boehl, ca. 1907. MHS Photographs and Prints.

With the ragtime background in place, the incoming talent entered an environment where music was an established feature of local culture. St. Louis musicians had easy access to pianos, and early St. Louis bluesmen such as Peetie Wheatstraw, Henry Brown, and Roosevelt Sykes honed their skills on the piano, which became a distinguishing feature of the St. Louis sound. Early guitar players such as Lonnie Johnson, Clifford Gibson, Big Joe Williams, and Henry Townsend also migrated to St. Louis, and the city's blues sound was characterized by piano/guitar combos during its formative years.

**African American workers in the Scullin Steel foundry.**
**Photograph by W. C. Persons, 1914–1919. MHS Photographs and Prints.**

Artists migrating to St. Louis could find work relatively easily in businesses such as factories and meat-packing plants. Blues legend Henry Townsend worked at a shoe-shine parlor (a front for a whiskey bootlegging operation), and he stated that around the Union Station area, it was easy for African Americans to find work at parlors, barbershops, and other similar service operations (Townsend 1999). Nightlife in the area thrived, and clubs, hotels, and sporting houses provided work opportunities in both St. Louis and East St. Louis during the 1920s and beyond. In the African American communities, musicians could easily congregate to play at house parties and in the streets, and a closely knit music scene developed (Townsend 1999). Incoming artists brought a diverse range of styles and backgrounds, and they shared their talents. Henry Townsend has stated that Roosevelt Sykes taught him certain songs on the piano in the 1920s, songs that Townsend eventually taught to Walter Davis in the 1930s. Musicians were in close proximity to each other, they learned from each other, and a blues sound began to develop that was unique to St. Louis (Townsend 1999; Davis 1995).

The most important figure of the early blues scene may have been Lonnie Johnson, who migrated to St. Louis from New Orleans in 1920. During the 1920s, Johnson performed regularly at the Booker Washington Theatre, where he won a blues contest several weeks in a row to earn a recording contract with Okeh Records (Oliver 1965). Johnson recorded several hits with vocalists such as Victoria Spivey and Clara Smith, and he's cited as a profound influence by both Elvis Presley and modern blues legend B. B. King (Davis 1995). Lonnie Johnson was the most influential guitarist of his time, and Henry Townsend idolized him. Inspired by Johnson, Henry Townsend went on to record in seven decades, and is still a central figure in the local blues scene.

**Henry Townsend in 2002.**
**Photo by Marilyn Wolfe, Natural Aspects Photography.**

Townsend was extremely active during the 1930s and 1940s, and during this era other great bluesmen continued to move into St. Louis and stay for a few years at a time. In the prewar era, legends such as Little Milton, Son House, Bukka White, Jimmy Rodgers, and Muddy Waters all lived in the area at some point. They could find work rather easily at places such as the Cartridge Factory, located at Goodfellow and Highway 70. Run by Augie Busch during the 1940s, the Cartridge Factory produced munitions for the war, and Muddy Watters, Son House, and other musicians worked there while contributing to the vitality of the local blues scene. African American neighborhoods continued to thrive both downtown and in East St. Louis, nightlife remained strong, and the music tradition was an established component of local culture. When combined with these factors, availability of work in places such as the Cartridge Factory helped make the city a viable option for traveling bluesmen.

The influx of talent continued during the 1950s and 1960s, when many of the genre's most legendary performers made St. Louis their home. Albert King moved to St. Louis in 1956, and he played his trademark Gibson "Flying V" guitar at the local clubs for almost ten years. Anyone could see Ike and Tina Turner for fifty cents at the Imperial Club in north St. Louis, where they were often joined by local mainstays Bennie Smith and Billy Peek. Aware of the success that Ike Turner enjoyed in St. Louis, Oliver Sain traveled in from Mississippi and began playing with Little Milton. Sain's career prospered and he decided to stay, becoming one of the city's most influential musicians, producers, and bandleaders.

During the 1950s and 1960s, many of St. Louis's most important musicians used their blues roots to explore emerging art forms such as rock n' roll and rhythm and blues, and St. Louis artists made landmark contributions to the history of American music. After establishing himself locally, for instance, Oliver Sain became nationally recognized as an R&B great. Chuck Berry and Johnnie Johnson played together in East St. Louis for years before they left and introduced the world to rock n' roll. Berry, Johnson, and Billy Peek toured the world together as rock n' roll pioneers, and all three musicians returned to St. Louis, where they've contributed to the local blues scene for three decades.

As R&B, soul, and rock n' roll emerged, the blues experienced a decline in the late 1960s and 1970s. In the late 1970s and 1980s, however, the blues became an increasingly popular choice for white "baby-boomer" audiences, who were inspired by the release of the *Blues Brothers* movie and turned off by the makeup-wearing glam artists that characterized the era's mainstream rock. Listening to the blues became a hip, trendy activity, and the Soulard neighborhood was the place to be. In Soulard, locals could jump from bar to bar and hear artists such as Doc Terry, Tommy Bankhead, Big George Brock, and the Soulard Blues Band all on the same night.

No one understands the Soulard neighborhood like Art Dwyer, a longtime resident who worked as a city police officer before founding the Soulard Blues Band in 1978. Dwyer reminisced with me about the explosion of blues in Soulard during the 1980s. For more than fifteen years, Billy Peek and the Soulard Blues Band were booked in stone at the Great Grizzly Bear. The two acts would alternate weekends, and the house was packed and rocking on a nightly basis. Mike & Min's on Geyer had the same commitment to the blues, and in 1979 the Soulard Blues Band played to raucous crowds every Friday and Saturday night for eighteen months, rarely leaving without performing two encores.

Throughout the 1980s, Tommy Bankhead was a weekend regular at Mike & Min's, and he became a St. Louis blues legend. Many current favorites, such as Rich McDonough, Eric McSpadden, and Alvin Jett, developed their skills by playing with Bankhead during the 1980s. In addition to Mike & Min's, other bars such as 1860's Hard Shell Café, Hammerstone's, Molly's, Hilary's (now Johnnie's), and the Soulard Ale House regularly featured blues acts. The clubs in Soulard were packed nightly, and the nightlife centered on the blues. During this time, clubs such as Blueberry Hill and Cicero's in the University City Loop also featured blues on regular basis. The blues were everywhere, and venues such as the Caravan Club at Delmar and Taylor, owned by harmonica legend Big George Brock, would often host six hundred people on a Saturday night. Doc Terry and Tommy Bankhead played at Sadie's on the north side, and you could also find blues at places such as Caleco's on Laclede Street, the Albert Moonlight Lounge on Martin Luther King Drive, Off Broadway, and Laclede's Landing, where the Soulard Blues Band was the house band at the River Rat (which eventually became Muddy Waters) for a brief period in the early 1980s.

With their popularity soaring in the 1980s, several local acts toured both nationally and in Europe. The Soulard Blues Band played festivals overseas, and Big Bad Smitty toured Europe with a band that included Bennie Smith. With the genre enjoying a resurgence, new bands were created. In 1985, Sharon Foehner decided that she wanted to play with Bennie Smith, who hadn't performed much during the 1970s. They created the now-legendary Bennie Smith and the Urban Blues Express, the only band in town guaranteed two weekend nights a month at BB's. Bennie Smith has become the face of the St. Louis blues: a patriarch who not only delivers great shows, but also serves as a valuable link between the future of the blues and the scene's rich history.

**Bennie Smith in 1994.**
**Photo by Joseph Frisch.**

Although Bennie continues to thrill on a regular basis, the blues resurgence of the 1980s has subsided. Today you're more likely to find DJs, jam bands, or alternative rock at the neighborhood bars in Soulard. Club owners have gone in a different direction, booking "newer" forms of music and entertainment in an effort to attract younger audiences. You won't find Bennie Smith on MTV, and most younger bar patrons don't appreciate the blues until they end up having a blast on the dance floor during one of Bennie's late-night sets. Several bars in Soulard that don't feature blues, such as Big Daddy's and McGurk's, attract hoards of young people on the weekends. As a result, other bars are attempting to follow this model. Club owners are naturally concerned with the bottom line, and although the decline of blues in Soulard and other neighborhoods is unfortunate, it is understandable.

Fortunately, there are clubs in St. Louis that remain devoted to the preservation and promotion of the local blues tradition. A few Soulard bars, such as the Blues City Deli and Hammerstone's, still feature the blues. The Venice Café hosts Bennie Smith every once in a while, and 1860's Hard Shell Café still books blues artists such as Marcel Strong, River City Blues Band, and Billy Barnett. Although the Great Grizzly Bear now books a wide variety of acts, it also features the Soulard Blues Band a few times each month. With the emphasis on blues declining in neighborhoods such as Soulard and the Loop, the South Broadway "Triangle" has emerged as the go-to area for St. Louis blues. Located across from Busch Stadium, BB's, Beale on Broadway, and the Broadway Oyster Bar continue to feature the area's top talent on a regular basis, and the Broadway Triangle thrives as a blues hotbed.

In 1976, St. Louisans Bob Burkhardt and Mark O'Shaughnessy converted a three-story hotel that had been a house of ill repute into BB's Jazz, Blues and Soups, now St. Louis's landmark blues club. Current owners O'Shaughnessy and John May live the blues: They're addicted to the music, and they're working hard to increase the local, national, and worldwide awareness of our city's music tradition. Although they book the nation's top touring acts on a regular basis, Friday and Saturday nights at BB's are reserved for local artists. The musicians receive a relatively sizeable portion of the door proceeds, which can add up on a weekend night in St. Louis, especially given the club's proximity to Busch Stadium.

BB's operates as a quasi-museum, filled with paintings, photographs, and artifacts that celebrate the contributions of St. Louis's most influential blues artists. Kevin Belford, a local artist and blues historian, contributed many of the works, and a series of Belford's lithographs line the back wall of the bar at BB's, immortalizing early St. Louis blues artists such as Henry Townsend, Peetie Wheatstraw, Big Joe Williams, Victoria Spivey, Lonnie Johnson, Walter Davis, and Roosevelt Sykes. BB's plans to expand in 2006, and the club will feature a second floor and a balcony that overlooks the stage. This expansion will allow the club to feature more exhibits and accommodate the increased downtown activity that the new baseball stadium promises to generate.

Located directly across the street, Beale on Broadway also features live music seven nights a week, and owner Bud Joestes is devoted to the blues. A great spot for open sit-ins, Beale on Broadway features an outdoor stage.

When the performers are outside, the music rings throughout the neighborhood, enhancing the allure of the neighborhood during the summertime. Across the street from the Beale, the Broadway Oyster Bar completes the Triangle. Although the club frequently books zydeco, funk, and jam bands, blues are still featured on a regular basis. Like the Beale, the Oyster Bar has a patio, making it an attractive summer spot. Wildly decorated, the bar has a New Orleans–style decor, and like BB's and the Beale, it attracts a diverse crowd. Everyone is welcome, and no one has to wait in line. There's no dress code in the Broadway Triangle, and the drinks are cheap and stiff. The three bars in the Broadway Triangle are keeping the blues scene alive, and the proximity to Busch Stadium creates a potent, distinctive sports-music combination that cannot be found in other cities.

Along with the clubs and bars, other local organizations support the area's blues culture. The St. Louis Blues Society, a nonprofit organization founded in 1984, remains committed to its mission of "preserving and perpetuating Blues music in and from St. Louis, while fostering its growth and appreciation." Led by President John May, the Blues Society emphasizes education and history, archiving the legacies of local artists. The leaders of the society conduct interviews, publish the *BluesLetter* quarterly magazine, archive oral histories, help artists record, and collect photographs and artifacts. When I approached Mark O'Shaughnessy to discuss this writing project, he immediately walked upstairs to his personal museum and retrieved a Henry Townsend CD and Townsend's autobiography, which he loaned to me without hesitation. Recently the Blues Society increased its preservation efforts by recruiting Kevin Belford to videotape Bennie Smith during shows at BB's. May and O'Shaughnessy plan to stream these shows from BB's over the Internet and broadcast them on TV, so that people around the world can enjoy frequent access to the St. Louis blues scene.

In addition to historical preservation, the Blues Society often organizes events aimed at increasing the consciousness of blues in the area. When St. Louis hosted the NCAA basketball Final Four in 2005, downtown St. Louis was flooded with more than 94,000 tourists. May organized a three-stage blues festival on Laclede's Landing that featured local artists exclusively, giving them an opportunity to showcase their talents to thousands of tourists. On the main stage, Rich McDonough delivered a jaw-dropping guitar display, and visiting basketball fans stopped their activity to watch in amazement. The concert closed with a set by Johnnie Johnson, which sadly turned out to be his last performance.

Rich McDonough. Photo by Molly Hayden.

When Johnson died, May planned a tribute concert in ten days, featuring a who's who of local blues artists that included Billy Peek and Chuck Berry, Johnson's fellow rock trailblazers. A perfect tribute to Johnson's legendary career, the sold-out concert highlighted the scope of Johnson's influence. The Blues Society also organizes Henry Townsend's annual star-studded birthday party and plans fund-raisers for programs such as the Blues Mission Fund, designed to support local artists and their families when they require financial assistance.

Perhaps the most important function of the Blues Society has been the organization of major St. Louis blues festivals. During the 1980s, the annual blues festival attracted enormous crowds, and the event became the third-largest blues festival in the world. In 1994, however, May stopped organizing the festivals, due to an inability to gain location permits from the City of St. Louis and a lack of sponsorship. With increased sponsorship (or even a start-up loan), the City could provide valuable support for a festival that would showcase one of the City's unique assets, attract massive numbers of people to downtown St. Louis, and generate nationwide interest in the City. Despite financial difficulties, the blues festival has re-emerged as a smaller, two-day event, and John May currently plans the Big Muddy Blues Festival in conjunction with Dawne Massey of Laclede's Landing. In 2005, the festival featured Bennie Smith,

Hidden Assets

Rich McDonough, Kim Massie, and several other local acts, along with nationally known figures Bo Diddley and Koko Taylor.

Several other organizations, such as STLBlues.net, also make valuable contributions to the vitality of the blues scene in St. Louis. Founded by blues lover Dave Beardsley in 2000, STLBlues.net features over six hundred pages of material, and the Web site's impact is verifiable: In 2004, StlBlues.net received over four million "hits" from Internet users. Visitors can read profiles and interviews to learn more about the musical backgrounds, philosophies, and influences of St. Louis's most prominent artists. Admirably, Beardsley posts these band profiles and interviews free of charge, giving musicians a valuable electronic promotional tool. In addition, the site provides links to Web sites for most of the area's local blues bands, news updates about blues-related topics, and reviews of CDs and live shows.

The *St. Louis Post-Dispatch* also makes valuable contributions to the blues scene: The paper does an excellent job of promoting and covering major events such as the Big Muddy Blues Festival, and writers such as Kevin Johnson often contribute blues-related pieces. There are those at the *Post-Dispatch* who understand and appreciate the St. Louis blues tradition, and the death of Johnnie Johnson brought out the best in the paper. The *Post* paid Johnnie a moving tribute, highlighting the accomplishments of an oft-overlooked artist and acknowledging his remarkable influence on the history of American rock n' roll.

In addition to these sources, other organizations continue to help expose blues music to the public. The record store Vintage Vinyl has always offered a strong selection of blues recordings, including releases from local artists such as the Soulard Blues Band and Bennie Smith, whose recent release *Shook Up* received critical acclaim both locally and nationally. In addition, local radio station KDHX (FM 88.1) continues to support the music. DJ Gabriel plays blues records from 12:30 to 5:30 a.m. on Tuesday mornings, and over the years he's developed friendships with many of the genre's most prominent artists. On Sunday nights, you can hear "Nothin' but the Blues" with Ron Edwards, a local historian and guitarist who's recorded with Henry Townsend. In addition to Edwards and Gabriel, Art Dwyer has his own show, "Blues in the Night." You can catch contemporary blues on "Soul Selector" with Papa Ray and a range of blues styles on "Blursday" with John McHenry and Denny Clancy. These programs often showcase historic recordings from early St. Louis blues artists, and KDHX currently broadcasts over the Internet, giving the music worldwide exposure.

In recent years, Jeremy Segel-Moss of the Bottoms Up Blues Gang has also worked hard to promote the blues. His band performs relentlessly, and their acoustic format allows them to play in a variety of clubs, raising consciousness of the blues in neighborhoods other than the Broadway Triangle. The band's work ethic inevitably draws attention to their albums, which feature cameos from legendary St. Louis artists. In addition, Segel-Moss is a regular contributor to *Playback* magazine, the *BluesLetter*, and STLBlues.net. Of all his contributions, Segel-Moss seems most proud of the Baby Blues Showcase, an annual event he began in 2002 to showcase younger blues artists who are critical to the survival of blues.

St. Louis has always had a vibrant scene and great talent. The city is a natural breeding ground for the blues, due to its location on the Mississippi River between Memphis and Chicago, status as a "gateway" to the West, railroad traffic, rich music tradition, and strong African American communities. In the eyes of many musicians and historians, however, the St. Louis blues scene has never received the national acclaim that it deserves. While the artists and clubs have always been world class, St. Louis's place in music history typically falls behind other cities such as New Orleans, Memphis, and Chicago, a phenomenon that most historians attribute to the city's lack of a major recording presence and music business infrastructure.

Musicians need to earn a living, and as blues evolved from folk art into big business, the opportunities to make records and profit lured many of them away. The city was loaded with artists and clubs, but without the big-time studios and business infrastructure, St. Louis did not receive the credit enjoyed by cities such as Chicago. A major label can distribute records throughout the world, promote artists, join artists with other influential musicians, and arrange an artist's tour. Without the industry here to support the scene, local artists lacked the advantages that high-profile legends such as Muddy Waters and Howlin' Wolf enjoyed in Chicago. As a result, many of these artists simply used St. Louis as a temporary home.

After World War II, when music industry entrepreneurs had more money at their disposal, many record labels were established in other cities. This never fully materialized in St. Louis, however, despite the city's deep talent base and central location. Many local artists and historians have suggested that if Berry Gordy had lived in St. Louis instead of Detroit, St. Louis could have easily been Motown. Instead, St. Louis didn't keep its talent around long enough for it to be recognized as one of the greatest blues cities. In the 1950s, Chuck Berry traveled from St. Louis to Chicago, where he met Muddy Waters and ended up recording "Maybelline" for Chess Records in 1955. Similarly, Albert King honed his craft for ten years in St. Louis, before eventually leaving to record with Stax Records in Memphis. After he signed with Stax, King's career skyrocketed. He teamed up with Booker T. & the MGs to create famous recordings such as "Born under a Bad Sign," and he became a national blues hero.

Many local artists believe that there are benefits to St. Louis's relative musical obscurity. Egos take a backseat to the art, and the artists have formed a close-knit community, based on respect for one another and the art form. They play for the love of the music; there's little competition over contracts, money, or gigs; and often local artists sit in with each other's bands. In fact, there are many nights where anyone with the inclination can come up and jam. Bennie Smith, the Soulard Blues Band, the Shakey Ground Blues Band, guitar player Brian Curran, and others all host open jam sessions, and they're happy to share the stage with their supporters.

In this cooperative environment, many artists have honed their craft by learning from others. It's become a St. Louis blues tradition—Henry Townsend taught songs to Walter Davis, Bennie Smith taught riffs to Ike Turner, and Alvin Jett developed by playing with Tommy Bankhead. More recently, the Bottoms Up Blues Gang formed after Jeremy Segel-Moss and singer Kari Liston discovered each other during sit-ins with Brian Curran and harmonica player Eric McSpadden. During our conversations, Segel-Moss emphasized the value of being able to play with those he admired, and he noted that if he asks politely, artists are willing to further his education. He's had Bennie Smith teach him riffs, Gus Thornton's sat in with the band, and the most recent album from the Bottoms Up Blues Gang, *2nd Set*, features cameos from Bennie, McSpadden, Sharon Foehner, Thornton, pianist Matt Murdick, harmonica legend Keith Doder, Tom Maloney, trumpeter Brian Casserly, and others. The band's experiences illustrate a St. Louis tradition: Local artists exude a heartfelt passion for the music, a reverence for its history, and a willingness to share it with their peers.

The local blues scene is a valuable local asset, and in addition to providing world-class entertainment for remarkably low prices, it also confers collateral advantages on the City of St. Louis. The blues clubs don't discriminate in any way, and they draw a diverse audience that typically doesn't develop elsewhere in St. Louis nightlife. The bars expose patrons to the contributions that African Americans have made to the history of music and our local culture. Whites and blacks perform together on stage, and listeners from a wide variety of backgrounds are unified by the power of great music. The blues venues also attract visitors to St. Louis, and tourists from all over the world are often spotted enjoying the scene at BB's. The St. Louis Convention and Visitors Commission (CVC) uses the blues tradition as a marketing tool in its efforts to attract conventions, business meetings, and visitors to the area. In fact, the St. Louis CVC has created marketing packets designed specifically to promote the local music scene.

What does the future hold? During the past several years, St. Louis has lost many influential blues leaders, such as Doc Terry, Tommy Bankhead, Oliver Sain, and Johnnie Johnson. Artists such as Henry Townsend, Bennie Smith, and Arthur Williams represent the city's last remaining links to the early roots, and as they grow older many local artists have expressed a concern about the future of the blues. Can newer blues artists possibly create similar music without having experienced the hardships, oppression, and sorrow that fueled the creation of the art form? Are younger African Americans interested in the blues in an era when hip-hop and its allure of fame and fortune dominate? These are legitimate concerns. Tom Maloney told me, however, that "the blues has never been the most popular selling music . . . but it has never died out. . . . it was created not for a commercial purpose—it was created out of the need . . . just sitting on the porch, getting away from the troubles of the day or their lives—it created something so potent, so relevant to the human condition, that it really spoke to the people." Maloney's comments echo the teachings of Henry Townsend: The blues is the truth. It's a genuine, heartfelt expression of the human condition, and the blues has endured for over one hundred years, while fads have come and gone. In St. Louis, the blues has endured without the promise and rewards of large-scale commercial success. Although the scene may be in transition, it will continue as long as musicians play with reverence for the music and an appreciation for those who created it.

Thanks to rich history, world-class artists who love the music, and the continuing efforts of local supporters, the blues scene has developed into a distinctive asset for the City of St. Louis. The blues culture distinguishes St. Louis from other metropolitan areas and is central to the area's identity. The talent is here, and business could follow. It's easy to envision a record label establishing a St. Louis presence, and acts like the Rich McDonough Band, Phat noiZ, and Kim Massie could succeed on national tours. If business and promotional leaders emerge, local artists could achieve new levels of success, both in St. Louis and nationwide. The local musicians have developed in a cooperative community, they love the music, and they understand the importance of history and tradition. Certainly, St. Louis artists could enjoy greater exposure without poisoning the sense of community this hidden asset has fostered.

Downtown St. Louis is growing, and recent development has created trendier nightlife options that present a crossroads for the blues scene. With herds of young people rediscovering the city and a new stadium being constructed, the overall perception of downtown as a viable nightlife option will evolve. Hopefully, all of this will steer more people to the Broadway Triangle every once in a while to experience something slightly different, cut loose in a diverse setting, and hear some amazing music. With its clubs, lounges, lofts, and sushi bars, St. Louis can imitate other cities. But even if other cities tried, they could never reproduce St. Louis's rich musical heritage. Hometown pride is powerful, and St. Louisans can find it in the blues.

**Kim Massie. Photo by Molly Hayden.**

## Acknowledgments

Much of the information in this chapter was obtained from conversations with artists and historians. Contributions were made by:

April 2005: Tom Maloney, John May, Rich McDonough

May 2005: Art Dwyer, Mary Hendron, Alvin Jett, Dawne Massey, Leroy Pierson, Bob Santelli, Jeremy Segel-Moss

June 2005: Kevin Belford, Gerald Early, Sharon Foehner, Eric McSpadden, Mark O'Shaughnessy, Billy Peek

September 2005: Kim Massie

### References

Davis, Francis. *The History of the Blues: The Roots, the Music, the People*. New York: Hyperion, 1995.

Handy, W. C. *Father of the Blues: An Autobiography*. Reprint. New York: Da Capo Press, 1991.

Oliver, Paul. *Conversation with the Blues*. Pittsburgh: Horizon Press, 1965.

Palmer, Robert. *Deep Blues*. New York: Penguin Books, 1982.

Townsend, Henry. *A Blues Life*. As told to Bill Greensmith. Champaign: University of Illinois Press, 1999.

# Chapter 7

# Cuttin´ Up 4 You: The Role of Barbershops in African American Communities

**Rod Brunson**

African American barbershops are important community institutions but are seldom included in contemporary discussions of neighborhoods. After reading this chapter, hopefully persons who have never stepped foot inside such establishments will recognize their relevance for generating social and political capital as well as collective efficacy within urban communities. To achieve this level of understanding, I use a qualitative approach, which allows me to figuratively prop open the doors of black barbershops, offering the reader a unique opportunity to experience the raised voices and boisterous laughter that result from spirited debates over contentious social issues and rapid-fire exchanges of stinging quips.

Media portrayals of African American barbershops have certainly documented the witty banter and lighthearted discussions that take place between barbers and patrons. And while these *are* characteristics of black barbershops, they are but a small part of the overall haircutting experience. This study examines in-depth the nature and meanings of key relationships that are developed and nurtured in this context and the implications they have for the larger community.

My findings are drawn from numerous hours of participant observation and many informal conversations with barbers in St. Louis. The analysis is also informed by my experience as a patron of several St. Louis black barbershops for the past twenty-five years. In addition, I offer a detailed case study of one barbershop to better illustrate key themes that consistently emerged during the course of this investigation.[1] Though I

---

[1] I had been a regular customer and visited the shop biweekly for approximately two and a half years prior to the start of the study. I thus had already established rapport not only with the staff, but also with many of the regular customers. Systematic observations were collected between February and September 2005.

make several references to the typical black barbershop, I am fully aware that some establishments may fit my representation better than others.

Scholars have long recognized the importance of local institutions as a means of promoting collective efficacy—the process by which neighborhood residents share responsibility for public order maintenance (Sampson, Raudenbush, and Earls 1997). However, collective efficacy is more likely to develop in communities where residents have strong ties to one another and neighborhood institutions. Thus researchers have also considered the extent to which local institutions (e.g., churches and schools) have influence over members of the community. The black barbershop is also a key component of neighborhood life and is therefore an important setting for the development and maintenance of collective efficacy.

As discussed previously, the relevance of African American barbershops has been recognized in popular culture, though media depictions have been limited in scope. However, the topic has received scant attention in the academic community, despite receiving in-depth coverage in black literature. In fact, the most notable sociological examination of black barbershops to date highlights its import as a setting for gender-role construction (see Franklin 1985). My purpose here, however, is to provide a deeper understanding of the role of African American barbershops beyond the provision of haircutting services in a hyper-masculine and jovial environment, to draw attention to the often-overlooked contributions they make.

# The Setting

The traditional barber's pole with its red, white, and blue striping is commonly used to distinguish barbershops from other unassuming structures in the neighborhood. While these poles are featured prominently on buildings that house many black barbershops, they are often secondary to other creative marketing strategies. Specifically, the storefronts of many barbershops feature large picture windows that effectively serve as mini-billboards to passersby. These windows have become innovative ways for shop owners to reach potential customers.

For example, one strategy involves writing the names and telephone numbers of neighborhood barbershops in colorful eye-catching script on the most visible window(s) of the business. At first glance, many of these

A picture window in a barbershop. Photograph by Allison Deutsch, 2005.

Mural advertising the availability of barbering services.
Photograph by Allison Deutsch, 2005.

windows may appear gaudy; however, the importance of assigning the right name and flavor to a shop cannot be overstated. Another approach involves the use of Afrocentric words in the business name to make it clear that the establishment caters to a particular demographic (i.e., African Americans) or specializes in particular hairstyles such as napps, locs, dreds, and twists. Whereas some shops simply bear the owner's name, other proprietors are much more creative. For instance, many shop owners use unique spellings of words and phrases to advertise their barbers' superior haircutting skills and tout the special attention their customers receive, for example, Unique Kutz, Starr Designs, So Crunk & So Kleen, and Platinum Stylz.

**View of Ruffino's workstation, featuring Afrocentric artwork.**
**Photograph by Allison Deutsch, 2005.**

The physical setup of the shop is particularly important. Specifically, barbers are the focal points because they are responsible for moderating public discussions. Barbers are also charged with keeping patrons on topic, introducing new subjects, and encouraging individuals who are noticeably silent to participate in conversations. There are typically two to four barber chairs that serve as the centerpieces of the main area. They are arranged parallel to one another and provide customers with an unobstructed view of the ongoing floor show. Rows of simple, uncovered chairs are positioned along the walls of the shop for customers. In addition, the center position of the barber chairs allows the stylists to subtly display their haircutting skills to onlookers. This is accomplished by using the swivel feature of the chairs to change the position of the customer as needed. Over time barbers become skilled at "working" the large mirrors that typically hang on the walls behind and in front of them. This enables barbers to fully participate in the shop's activities without compromising the quality of their work.

Photographs of distinguished patrons and celebrities are commonly featured in many black barbershops. In addition, national African American civil rights activists, businessmen, athletes, and public officials are prominently displayed on the walls and mirrors, including figures like W. E. B. Du Bois, Marcus Garvey, John H. Johnson, Muhammad Ali, Michael Jordan, and Mayors Tom Bradley and Harold Washington. Most owners are very particular about the pictures they exhibit and note that they feature only pictures of individuals whom they hold in high regard. In fact, one barber refers to the wall of his shop (where photos hang) as the "wall of greatness." However, the photographs have a dual purpose. In addition to celebrating the extraordinary achievements of African American icons, the pictures are also intended to convey to customers that a particular shop is a safe and positive place for community residents. In particular, proprietors believe that undesirables are not comfortable in shops where social consciousness is promoted and as a result they will elect to go elsewhere.

**Wall of pictures of African American barbershop patrons and icons. Photograph by Allison Deutsch, 2005.**

Owing to the relevance of the barbershop as an important community institution, there are usually bulletin boards or other designated areas where patrons are allowed to post a variety of announcements (e.g., employment/real estate opportunities, church events, business cards, and various advertisements for services). Most shops are typically clean, except the area of the floor directly beneath the barbers' chairs. Young male patrons (ages thirteen to fifteen) are often informally employed to sweep between haircuts and perform other light housekeeping tasks (emptying garbage, cleaning mirrors, and running errands to replenish supplies). These youths are sometimes paid but typically receive either discounted or free haircuts in exchange for their services.

The job of "helper" is highly coveted and affords the holder high status, as it pays dividends far beyond the meager financial compensation. Compared to their peers, helpers are poised to form stronger social bonds to barbers and regulars, which results in increased mentoring opportunities. However, in addition to performing their barbershop duties well, helpers are expected to get good grades, obey their parents, and refrain from participating in delinquent or illegal activities. Those who are found in violation of these informal rules are counseled and warned that they run the risk of being replaced if the misconduct continues.

Local newspapers are ordinarily provided for patrons. However, magazines are more commonplace, and the most recent issues are typically neatly displayed in fabricated wooden racks or stands. The subject matter of the magazines is diverse and includes fashion, finances, politics, sports, and travel. There is usually at least one television set and stereo system. The television and music programming are typically influenced by clients' entertainment preferences. Many shops have modest kitchen and bathroom facilities located in the rear. Almost all shop owners discourage the use of the business line for personal calls, and therefore quite a few have pay telephones installed on the premises.

# Conversations with St. Louis Barbers

My conversations with barbers were loosely structured interviews in which they were free to elaborate on any subjects and introduce their own topics. However, I purposely steered conversations toward barbers' perceptions of the role their shops play in the black community in St. Louis. I also asked numerous questions about barbers' relationships with their clients. I took brief but detailed handwritten notes during the discussions and inserted supplemental information from memory immediately after leaving the shops. The length of conversations varied but typically lasted between one and two hours.

The majority of barbers I spoke with considered barbering a high form of service to the community requiring not only skill but also the utmost respect for self and others. In fact, most barbers were adamant that the profession involves much more than cutting hair. Specifically, several explained that they serve many roles in the neighborhood, including mentor, financial adviser, clergyman, lawyer, and relationship counselor. Barbers added that because clients tend to entrust them with very personal information, they have an obligation not to engage in gossip. They were insistent that even the slightest breach in confidence would inevitably lead to a loss in clientele.

Several barbers emphasized their informal roles as father figures for young males in the community—especially those who did not have relationships with their biological fathers. For instance, one barber remarked, "A lot of kids don't have fathers, and the shop gives them opportunities to have positive interactions with *real* black men." Likewise, numerous barbers remarked that many of their relationships with customers, who are now young adults, began twenty or more years ago. In fact, the majority of barbers noted that the black barbershop has always been a place where young men gather and learn about life from elders in the community. In addition, many barbers noted that quite a few of their current customers had "grown up" in the shop and were therefore considered part of their extended families. As a result, barbers reported having experienced births, weddings, graduations, and deaths alongside many of their longtime patrons.

Overall, the barbers I spoke with maintained that they are dedicated to making community residents feel important and appreciated while providing them with superior hair-care services. For example, one barber noted, "You can go anywhere and get a haircut, people who come *here* desire and are given more." Likewise, many barbers offered the longevity of their businesses and sustained relationships with clients as evidence of their unique contributions to the community. Barbers consistently mentioned that their shops allowed persons who had moved away from the old neighborhood to stay connected to childhood friends and neighbors, either through direct contact or by learning of their whereabouts and well-being from others.

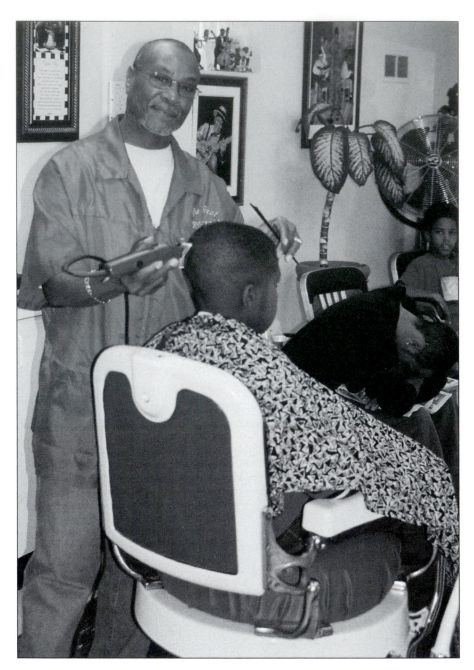

**Ruffino cuts a young patron's hair while other customers wait.
Photograph by Allison Deutsch, 2005.**

Most shop owners proudly mentioned that their clientele was composed of individuals from different social classes and were steadfast in their position that such diversity ultimately benefits the entire community. Specifically, they believed that if a shop maintains a relaxed and positive atmosphere, customers of varying backgrounds would be encouraged to share their unique experiences, skills, and talents with others. Several barbers commented that on numerous occasions customers unexpectedly learned that another patron could assist them with a particular problem. In fact, one barber is known to often proudly remark, "You never know who you might be sitting next to in *here*."

Several barbers likened their shops to "country clubs for regular folks" where everyone is made to feel welcome. One barber explained that clients fall into two categories: those who are in dire need of information or solutions to problems and those who possess remedies. Likewise, another barber explained that members of his profession must act as community developers to facilitate the exchange of "antidotes for illnesses."

Barbers highlighted the role shops play in patrons' ability to form and maintain individual-level social networks, thereby resulting in higher levels of collective efficacy among community residents. However, they also recognized that as local institutions, barbershops were well integrated into the larger business community. Specifically, barbers explained how their shops contributed to the economic stability of several nearby establishments (e.g., beauty supply outlets, take-out restaurants, and corner stores).

**View of neighboring businesses that are frequented by customers of Shegog's. Photograph by Allison Deutsch, 2005.**

# Shegog's: A Case Study

As mentioned earlier, portions of the data presented in this chapter result from systematic observations conducted at a particular black barbershop—Shegog's. Therefore the following case study highlights particular topics that emerged repeatedly during the course of my investigation. Charles and Ron, both African American, are barbers at Shegog's. Charles is the proprietor and is middle aged. He has been a barber for over three decades and has operated his own shop for the past twenty-two years. Shegog's has been in its current location for the past twelve years. The former site was located in the same community, but several blocks to the east.

**Ron (left) and Charles outside of Shegog's.**
**Photograph by Allison Deutsch, 2005.**

Charles is extremely intelligent and well read, which allows him to speak comfortably on a wide range of topics. He is very open about his lack of formal education but stresses his passion for acquiring knowledge. In fact, Charles proudly displays whatever book he is currently reading on the countertop directly behind his chair. He insists that he takes it upon himself to be well versed regarding a variety of contemporary topics because many of his clients "are working-class people" and often do not have time to read. Charles therefore believes that it is his duty to help customers realize how current events affect their lives.

Ron is very affable and challenges himself to improve spiritually. He is in his early thirties and has worked in Shegog's the entire time it has been at the current location. Ron notes that he continually encourages customers to embrace faith. He contends that the barbering profession relies heavily on the concept of faith. For instance, he states that barbers are unable to determine who is going to come through the door on any given day. Thus, a steady income is not guaranteed, and this makes it difficult to manage one's personal finances. However, Ron advises that he has simply decided to have faith that everything will work out—and it has for the past twelve years.

**View of Shegog's, facing north. Photograph by Allison Deutsch, 2005.**

Whereas patrons of Shegog's are predominantly black males, they are diverse in age, including community members from eight to eighty-eight. They represent diverse social classes as well.[2] Many occupations are represented among clients. These include politicians, academicians, doctors, police officers, businessmen, government employees, laborers, students, and teachers. A by-product of racial segregation in housing is that it increases the probability of middle- and lower-class blacks living in close proximity to one another (see Pattillo-McCoy 1999) and frequenting the same neighborhood institutions. This is the case with Shegog's. This

---

[2] Women typically are not customers, but occasionally accompany younger male children in the evenings or on Saturdays. There are a few female clients who receive limited services, such as eyebrow waxing or hair lining.

situation provides support for the view that barbershops are environments highly conducive to the development of collective efficacy.

**Negotiating the Shop**

There are several informal rules and customs governing conduct in Shegog's. These rules are seldom articulated unless they are violated, but over time patrons come to understand them. For example, first-time customers rarely participate in conversations unless one of the barbers invites them to do so. However, if a regular patron accompanies a new customer, the new customer is allowed to bypass the rule. First-time customers also refrain from laughing too hard or long at jokes told at the expense of regular customers, as they have not established the necessary social capital.

There is also an informal and rather sophisticated system of acquiring services. For example, customers are not assigned numbers; however, it is a shared responsibility between the customer and the barbers to keep track of the order in which services will be provided. It is also preferable, whenever possible, for customers to sit in the area of the shop closest to their barber's chair. However, new patrons are required to indicate (either verbally or by gesturing) which barber they prefer when their turn comes. There is also a matter of etiquette after one has established a relationship with a particular barber. Specifically, it is considered an insult if a patron switches barbers without first diplomatically explaining the circumstances surrounding the decision to the former barber.

There are no signs barring particular types of behaviors. However, customers adhere to informal and unspoken codes governing their conduct. For instance, barbers and patrons typically do not use profanity or offensive language. Rather, a second language of clever code words is used when they want to comment about sexually explicit or otherwise sensitive matters. This typically occurs in the presence of women, children, or unfamiliar patrons.

All transactions are handled in cash, and there is no visible cash register. Nor is a price list posted anywhere on the premises. If fees are discussed it is done so privately, between the patron and his barber, but typically they are not discussed at all. Most regular customers have established a price with their barber over time and simply tender payment by handing the barber currency. When required, change is given from the barber's pocket. The absence of a cash register and price list is characteristic of Charles's view that Shegog's is not merely a retail establishment where services are bought, but a place where ongoing social relationships are fostered.

Charles jokes with a customer while cutting his hair. Photograph by Allison Deutsch, 2005.

## The Functions of Social Interactions

As Charles suggested, the barbershop is a site for education and discussion of current events and their impact on the black community. Nonetheless, it is also a place for personal counsel for individual patrons. Public conversations are lighthearted, and even the most spirited debates tend to be peppered with humor. Customers are free to discuss any topic but recognize that others enjoy the privilege to aggressively challenge views that they do not agree with. The sometimes intense nature of these conversations provides support for what many in the black community already know. That is, similar to other racial groups, there are diverse views among black citizens regarding a host of topics spanning politics, religion, education, and crime control. The diversity of clients' backgrounds affords patrons opportunities to become better informed on a wide range of topics. In fact, Charles and Ron frequently call upon customers who have expertise concerning particular issues to take command of these discussions.

It is not uncommon for patrons to occasionally offer outlandish comments regarding a particular situation. However, it is sometimes difficult to determine whether the speaker believes what he has said or is simply interested in introducing a controversial topic. Also, customers rarely pass up an opportunity to draw attention to some celebrity who is in the media spotlight for some recent scandal or legal troubles (for instance, R. Kelly, Mike Tyson, Kobe Bryant, Michael Jackson, or Bill Cosby). Whereas popular culture generally highlights this type of "barbershop talk," such portrayals generally fail to recognize discussions of complex social issues that also occur in this context. As a result, they unwittingly belittle the role of barbershops in black communities.

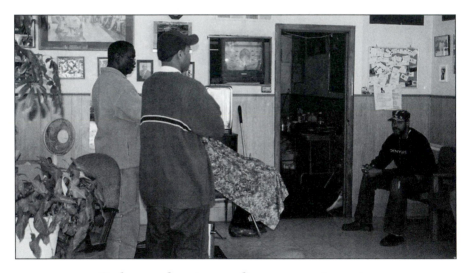

**Barbers and customers discuss current events.**
**Photograph by Allison Deutsch, 2005.**

Many conversations taking place in Shegog's concern social problems that disproportionately affect the black community. A majority of patrons link these situations to the callousness of local and national politicians whom they frequently and openly lambaste for ignoring poor communities. A number of customers are particularly critical of the Bush administration, which they perceive as being especially indifferent to the concerns of minority citizens. Patrons also speculated about the changing landscape of politics in America as the following exchange illustrates:

*Barber*: Condoleezza Rice is the answer for Hillary Clinton.

*Customer One*: Do you think they'll get her to run?

*Barber*: Right now she's running for her life over in the Gaza Strip. They got serious security around her.

The conversation continued:

*Barber*: Where is the vice president during all this [conflict in the Gaza Strip]? They hide him like he the president.

*Customer Two*: Shit, you mean he ain't? [Laughter erupts.]

Patrons also expressed their frustration with what they perceived as apathy in the black community concerning politics. Specifically, a number of patrons commented that "black folk" should pay better attention to political decisions that have the potential to dramatically change their lives. The following exchange is illustrative:

*Barber*: What's not being talked about in the black community is Clarence Thomas's chance of becoming chief justice of the Supreme Court.

*Customer*: Why would you think that would be talked about in the *black* community? [Laughter erupts.]

Patrons were also critical of those within the community whose actions were considered unacceptable. For example, customers frequently chided some young black men for their apparent indifference toward their children. During several conversations, older male customers remarked that young black men need to fully embrace old-school ethics regarding hard work and sacrifice if they intend on making anything of themselves:

*Barber*: These little dudes today too busy trying to be all big showing off their expensive clothes, cars, and jewelry to take care of their kids.

> *Customer*: Man, my wife works with these youngsters who don't want
> to do nothing for themselves. They always talk about how they ain't
> got this or ain't got that but they don't wanna do what it takes to get
> ahead. I lived downtown for five years and took the bus every day to
> work way out in the county.

Customers also expressed their frustration with the "supposed" leadership
in the black community. Specifically, many patrons commented that the so-
called spokespersons fail to represent the views of the community but are
perhaps more palatable than others to the general public:

> *Customer One*: We seem to have a shortage of black leaders. I mean *real*
> black leaders, not the  ones that are selected for us. It seems that the
> only leaders that we are allowed to have are those that are acceptable
> to mainstream America. It's been that way for as long as I can
> remember. In fact, my daddy would often make the same comment.

> *Customer Two*: And why is it that our leaders are always named
> Reverend something? Churches are among the most profitable
> institutions in our communities and look at the conditions that most
> black folks live in. Where does all that money that gets collected on
> Sunday go?

Many conversations, even those that were seemingly unrelated, steered
to race. For example, customers discussed why black public officials and
celebrities were always under attack by representatives of the criminal
justice system and the media. Importantly, however, discussions of race
were not consumed by viciousness or conspiracy theories. Instead, they
involved a sociological approach toward understanding the influence of
race—particularly in St. Louis. There was often a lack of consensus among
patrons regarding whether substantial progress had been made locally or
nationally regarding race relations or racial equality. However, even those
who agreed that progress had been made differed in their opinions
regarding the degree to which things had improved.

A number of customers commented that because of the legacy of racism
in America, black people would always be viewed negatively and therefore
treated poorly. The following excerpt is from a conversation regarding
Hurricane Katrina and the subsequent flooding in New Orleans:

> *Customer*: The media had better hurry up and put a white face on the
> disaster in New Orleans if they expect white folks to donate money.
> So far they've been showing pictures of black folks trying to survive.
> And yes, there is a difference between looting and trying to provide
> food and clothing for your family.

Excerpts of public conversations emphasize the role of barbershops as important black community institutions. In particular, they highlight that the neighborhood barbershop is a place where individuals from different social strata converge and exchange information and viewpoints. Last, the barbershop creates an environment in which patrons feel comfortable expressing opinions about a number of sensitive subjects without fear of reprisal.

Public conversations, while revealing, do not allow us to fully appreciate the multifaceted role of the black barbershop. Public conversations tend not to be of a personal nature. Patrons seldom disclose any sensitive information about themselves in that context. Private conversations between barbers and patrons play an equally important role in the contributions of the barbershop to the community, because it is in this context that patrons can discuss their private problems, and seek advice and resolution.

I explored the nature of private conversations between barbers and patrons with Charles and Ron as well as with other barbers. And while they did not reveal any identifying information about specific customers—given the confidential nature of these exchanges—they did explain that more personal conversations are likely to take place when there are fewer people in the shop or during one-on-one conversations while barbering services are being rendered. This context affords the patron confidentiality, as these conversations are not held above a whisper. These conversations involve disclosures regarding, for example, marital problems, health issues, employment losses, and financial setbacks. It is during this exchange that the more intimate counseling aspects of barbering takes place.

# Conclusion

Scholars have long recognized that community institutions play key roles in helping shape residents' lives by promoting collective efficacy. The current study extends this line of research by considering the extent to which African American barbershops are also important for neighborhood stability. My goal was to offer an in-depth examination of relationships operating in black barbershops. By using qualitative methods, this study provides unique insights into the nature and meanings of interactions between patrons and barbers.

Variation in neighborhood conditions has been linked to observed differences in the capacity of communities to achieve solidarity among residents through formal and informal networks (see Bursik and Grasmick 1993). Therefore, it makes sense to examine not only the existence but also the quality of social bonds in a particular context. My findings suggest that black barbershops facilitate the formation and growth of strong social ties which have consequences for the larger neighborhood. In fact, barbershops appear to be among the more resilient institutions in many urban communities—even those that have been "run down" by worsening social conditions. Recall the barbers' discussions about the length of time they had been in business and the number of years their relationships with clients spanned.

Media accounts of African American barbershops have narrowly focused on the shop as theatre. However, the current study highlights that black barbershops provide benefits to patrons that extend far beyond providing entertainment. Specifically, the barbershop functions as a temporary refuge from daily pressures and allows patrons to obtain counsel and acquire knowledge regarding a number of important topics.

Like many U.S. cities over the past few decades, St. Louis has experienced a steady migration of its black citizenry from the inner city to the suburbs. It seems reasonable to consider whether continued population shifts in this direction will cause neighborhood-based barbershops to follow their customers. In addition to the economic loss, such moves may result in fragmented or weakened social ties among community residents. However, this study suggests that the social bonds developed and nurtured in black barbershops are strong enough to survive suburbanization. As I have shown, African American barbershops are important non-traditional local institutions rich in history and tradition. Therefore, similar to their elders, future generations of black males will come of age in shops while acquiring the many intangible benefits that the setting provides.

**References**

Bursik, Robert, Jr., and Harold Grasmick. *Neighborhoods and Crime: The Dimensions of Effective Community Control.* New York: Lexington Books, 1993.

Franklin, C. W. "The Black Male Urban Barbershop as a Sex-Role Socialization Setting." *Sex Roles* 12 (1985): 965–979.

Pattillo-McCoy, Mary. *Black Picket Fences: Privilege and Peril among the Black Middle Class.* Chicago: University of Chicago Press, 1999.

Sampson, R. J., S. W. Raudenbush, and F. Earls. "Neighborhoods and Violent Crime: A Multilevel Study of Collective Efficacy." *Science* 277 (1997): 918–924.

# Chapter 8

# Riverian Revelation

**Mark Tranel**

The river is a constant reminder that St. Louis has always been part of something larger than itself.—*Katharine Corbett*, St. Louis Currents, 1997

In the twentieth century St. Louis acknowledged its legacy to great rivers by building what is arguably its most prominent architectural asset, the Gateway Arch. It took more than thirty years to realize the vision of what today is a large, public, open space on the downtown St. Louis riverfront.

The park for the Arch grounds was created by the demolition of forty city blocks of warehouse and other commercial buildings. After several years of effort St. Louis civic leaders were successful in petitioning the federal government to designate the area a national historical site in 1935. The site was cleared by 1942.[1] The privately funded Jefferson National Expansion Memorial Association selected the design for the Arch and its surroundings in 1947. With the federal government paying 80 percent of the cost, the Arch was completed in 1963.

This was actually a fairly quick turnaround compared to the development of one of the metropolitan area's most hidden assets. St. Louis is famous for being founded at the confluence of the Mississippi and Missouri rivers. But connected to these major continental waterways are 170 tributaries, a combined 2,100 stream miles. The region[2] is literally laced with riverian space. These watercourses have, however, long been overlooked as

---

[1] This was not the first time this area was cleared. The Great St. Louis Fire of 1849 burned practically to the ground essentially the same area later cleared for the Arch grounds.

[2] For purposes of this chapter, the St. Louis region will be considered the City of St. Louis and seven surrounding counties: in Missouri—Franklin, Jefferson, St. Louis, and St. Charles counties; in Illinois—Madison, Monroe, and St. Clair counties. The 2003 U.S. Census Bureau definition of the St. Louis metropolitan area includes fifteen counties and one city, but the other eight counties are not involved in the events or projects discussed here.

resources to community, health, and property value (Missouri Department of Conservation 2004). Many have been encapsulated in pipes, lined with concrete, or just disappeared altogether when filled in (Corbett 1997).

**Aerial view of St. Louis riverfront and city looking northwest toward the Gateway Arch. Photograph by Ted McCrea, 1969. MHS Photographs and Prints.**

# Riverian Abuse

St. Louis for generations has treated its riverian environment as one of two things: a disposable resource or an impediment to development. The earliest abuse of riverian flora started about two hundred years ago. Rivers and streams were the highways of the age of the steamboats. Much has been written about the contribution steamboats made to the growth of St. Louis (Primm 1998). Generally overlooked, though, is the impact steamboats had on the environment. A great deal of the landscape adjacent to waterways was deforested through the practice then known as "wooding" (Norris 1997). Steamboats used wood for fuel—a prodigious amount of wood.

By the mid-nineteenth century the port of St. Louis was second only to New York in volume of cargo. There were more than seven hundred steamboats providing daily service in the vicinity of St. Louis. The early boats were small and burned about 12 to 24 cords of wood a day. By 1860 the boats had grown much larger, daily burning 50 to 75 cords of wood. Harvesting approximately 44,000 cords of wood a day from the easily accessible land adjacent to the riverbanks had severe consequences. With no tree cover and active root systems, large areas of wildlife habitat were destroyed and erosion gradually affected the river channel (Norris 1997).

**View looking north up the Mississippi River toward the Eads Bridge at St. Louis. Wood engraving, 1887. MHS Photographs and Prints.**

The era of the steamboats ended in the 1880s. By then the population of St. Louis was about 400,000, having grown from 5,000 when the first steamboat landed in 1817. As the city grew in population, it grew in geography, spreading north, south, and west from the riverfront. Everywhere development went it encountered the tributary system that flowed into the major rivers.

Development creates impervious surfaces (streets, parking lots, and rooftops) and compacted earth that sheds rainwater rather than absorbing and storing it. This causes storm water to flow faster and in greater volume. Streams become deeper, wider, and straighter, causing ecological deterioration and property damage to streamside property and roadways. The responses vary from diversion and channelization to damming and piping, any of which eradicates the natural value of the riverian landscape (Missouri Department of Conservation 2004).

While largely devaluing riverian space, the urban development process always has included an allocation of open space (Garvin and Berens 1997). In the late nineteenth and early twentieth centuries, open space took the form of a few large regional parks (e.g., Forest Park and Tower Grove Park) and a larger number of small neighborhood parks. Of the 99 parks[3] in the City of St. Louis, for example, only 29 are larger than 10 acres. A majority of the parks are small neighborhood oases, more green spots than green space. These areas were considered important as much for what they weren't as for what they were. Urban development from 1880 to 1920 was physically dense, with most households living in multi-tenant buildings. Factories and other commercial uses were integrated into the landscape, not highly segregated as later became the practice. Under these conditions city parks, even if a few acres, were a relief from the built environment.

Open space is a critical asset in a metropolitan area, although its value in America has not been appreciated until the late twentieth century. In *The Benefits of Open Space* Leonard Hamilton details biological, ecological, economic, and psychological benefits (Hamilton 1997). But two trends occurred during the 1990s that changed the perception of what type of open space is most beneficial in metropolitan areas. First of all, recreational usage evolved (Kent and Madden 1998). Large numbers of people took up outdoor activities such as bicycling, jogging, inline skating, and cross-county skiing. These activities required a different type of facility than the small neighborhood park. A fairly extensive linear park is most attractive to these open-space users. There was some interest in promoting these activities not only for recreational or physical fitness but also as alternatives to dependency on automobile transportation. A change in federal law even allocated limited funding for development of infrastructure for these purposes (Shriver 1998). The second trend was an urban renaissance. Many older central cities had been losing population for decades, but in the 1990s empty nesters and young professionals began taking up residence in cities, and the existing structure of small, disconnected open spaces did not meet the needs of their active lifestyle.

---

[3] There are 99 parks owned and maintained by the City Department of Parks (2,642.2 acres/26 acre average). There are 9 other parks with various forms of ownership and maintenance. By contrast, in St. Louis County there are 73 parks (approximately 12,000 acres/164 acre average) owned and maintained by the County and another 290 parks (3,618 acres/12 acre average) owned and maintained by fifty-nine municipalities. In St. Charles County there are 8 parks (1,655.5 acres/206 acre average) owned and maintained by the County and 46 parks (1,801.5 acres/39 acre average) owned and maintained by seven municipalities. Three of the St. Charles County government parks are under development as of mid-2005 (1,013 acres). In addition the Missouri Department of Natural Resources has 6 parks in the three counties. The Missouri Department of Conservation owns approximately 13,000 acres in its St. Louis region, which includes Jefferson County.

**Aerial view of Forest Park looking east toward Kingshighway. Photograph by W. C. Persons, ca. 1920s. MHS Photographs and Prints.**

Park, recreation, and landscape planners began to realize that the means to respond to these trends circulated throughout urban areas. Metropolitan St. Louis, like many other regions, began not only to recognize that a connected network of open space is an asset, but also to capitalize on that asset (Fabos 1996).

## What Is a Greenway?
While the Gateway Arch is a popular attraction, drawing over 4 million visitors a year, its open-space setting has the challenge faced by many urban parks—access. While not convenient, there is vehicular and pedestrian access to the Arch park grounds. Much of the riverian open space throughout the rest of the metropolitan area is either fenced off, behind private property, or literally built over.

Lack of access in the St. Louis region to the major rivers and their tributaries and the need for a regional approach to open-space planning and development are both issues that have been long discussed. The U.S. Army Corps of Engineers prepared a 1977 report that documented needs existing at that time and projected future needs for the then-eight-county St. Louis MSA. Regarding use of the major rivers, particularly the Mississippi, the report stated, "Public access to the Mississippi is limited within the urbanized area and its recreational values have been largely ignored" (U.S. Army Corps of Engineers 1977, 65).

One approach adopted in a growing number of metropolitan areas that makes a connection between people and rivers is the development of parks known as greenways (Little 1995). Greenways are linear open spaces or parks along rivers, ridgelines, or historic infrastructure corridors such as canals or railroads that connect people with places and provide opportunities for recreation, conservation, and economic development (Lindsey 2003). Charles Little defines a greenway as "a linear open space established along . . . a natural corridor, such as a riverfront, stream valley, or ridgeline" (Schwarz 1993, xv). Searns (1995) delineates three generations in the evolution of greenways. In the "ancestral" period (pre-1700s to the 1960s) boulevards and parkways were "greened" roads that served vehicular traffic. The second generation (the 1960s to mid-1980s) shifted to linear parks that prohibited motorized vehicles from recreational access to rivers, streams, and abandoned rail beds. In the current generation (since the mid-1980s) greenways are "multi-objective" corridors designed to enhance water quality, reduce flood damage, and provide educational opportunity in addition to serving as recreational facilities.

St. Louis experienced all three of these generations but appears poised to be more successful in the development of third-generation greenways than it ever was in the first two.

# Historical Roots

The idea of a linear network of open space is not new in St. Louis. There have been multiple plans which date back almost one hundred years.

### 1907 Public Reservation District
In 1907 the Civic League, a booster organization, prepared a plan for capital improvements primarily in the City of St. Louis, but incorporating St. Louis County in some of its elements. One of those elements was a proposed Public Reservation District (Greater St. Louis Committee

1914). The District would have included St. Louis City and County in a parks district. The St. Louis manifestation of the "ancestral" period in Searns's evolution of greenways, the Outer Park Plan for the District would have developed an interconnected network of parks and greenways along a radius roughly sixteen miles from the St. Louis riverfront. The network included parkways to connect Meramec Highlands in south St. Louis County to Creve Coeur Park to a greenway running along the Missouri River bluffs above Holmes and Charbonnier islands in north St. Louis County (Map 1). "An extensive park and parkway system is all the more important in an inland city like St. Louis, which is situated far from the invigorating effects of the lake or ocean breezes and the natural attractiveness of a broad water-front. What the inland city lacks in these natural features it must make up in beautiful parks and drives" (Civic League 1907).

St. Louis doesn't have beaches, and it doesn't have mountains. What it does have is thousands of miles of waterfront property along an extensive network of rivers and streams.

**Map 1. Map of St. Louis City and County**

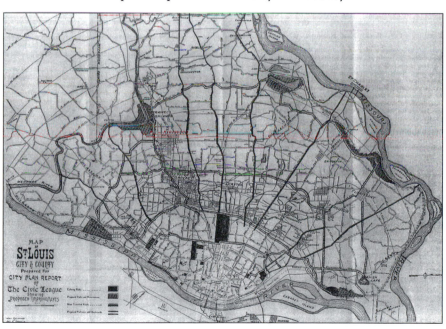

Source: Civic League of St. Louis.

The motivation to establish the District was a reflection of two trends. From 1890 to 1910 the population of the City of St. Louis increased by 50 percent, approaching 700,000 residents. In the process it became, at that time, the fourth-largest city in America. The growth was accommodated by very dense urban development and there was increasing concern over preservation of areas of open space. The rate of growth and the density of development drove up land prices, causing the fear that if land was not acquired in advance of development, it would become too expensive to acquire for open-space use. Other states at this same time were enabling the creation of metropolitan parks districts (Metropolitan Research and Services Center of Washington 2004).

The Public Reservation District failed to become a reality because of legal and political obstacles. During its 1909 session, the Missouri legislature approved a bill permitting the City and County to create the District. When the issue was brought to voters in November 1910, it failed in both the City and County. Then in 1912 an initiative secured signatures on a petition seeking another authorization from the legislature for a District vote. That year the lower house, then called the House of Delegates, refused to authorize an election, largely because of the rejection of a park district proposal just two years earlier. In 1913 legislation to establish a district was introduced but never voted on due to a clerical error.

Also in 1913 the Missouri Supreme Court ruled against the establishment of such districts: "No two adjoining counties could, even by vote of its citizens, create a new general taxing district" (Greater St. Louis Committee 1914). In 1915 the Greater Saint Louis Committee, with representatives of eight civil and commercial organizations, attempted without success to have enabling legislation adopted.

Rejection by voters in 1910 and the Supreme Court in 1913 had more influence over the legislators than petitions from business interests. Thus yearly in the twentieth century repeated efforts to establish a regional network of open space failed in the democratic process.

**The Gateway Discovery Trail**
In the mid-1970s another proposal was advanced for development of a multi-jurisdictional, linear open space. In 1974 East-West Gateway Coordinating Council proposed the Gateway Discovery Trail as a 230-mile corridor encircling St. Louis. That proposal was supplemented in 1975 with a plan for a metropolitan trail system.

As a planning agency, East-West Gateway had no dedicated source of funding for the proposed trail and no authority for implementing development of the system. It relied on ad hoc action by county and municipal governments.

**Map 2. Proposed Gateway Discovery Trail**

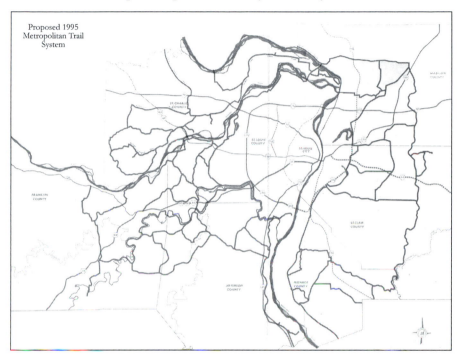

Proposed 1995
Metropolitan Trail
System

Source: East-West Gateway Coordinating Council.

The Gateway Discovery Trail was noted among recommendations for a Regional Park and Conservation System in a 1977 U.S. Army Corps of Engineers Water Resources Investigation. The St. Louis Metropolitan Area Study included proposals for conservation areas, forest preserves, and greenways as the framework for an area-wide park and recreation strategy. Here again, the lack of an implementing entity stalled any action on the Corps' proposal.

# Riverian Ascension

St. Louis's return to the rivers started in the mid-1990s and proceeded through four phases. Robert Olshansky identified three characteristics as necessary for creating parks in cities. These include citizen action, local sources of private and public funding, and professional planning (Olshansky 2003). Each of these characteristics was present in and important to the success of each phase. Built on a foundation of these factors, a vigorous regional commitment evolved to utilize these resources to enhance economic development, ensure environmental stewardship, and enrich social capital (Figure 1).

**Figure 1. Funding Chart**

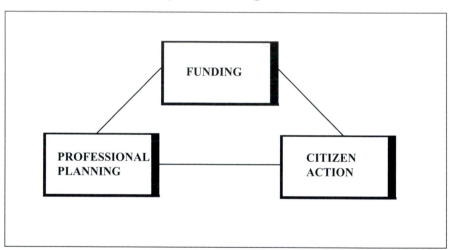

First of all, each phase of the process had adequate funding for a full-time professional staff for transitional organizations (*St. Louis Business Journal* 1999). Second, each phase engaged citizens in the earliest stages of the decision-making process. And finally, each phase engaged professional experts in a defined aspect of the initiative. One of the successful outcomes (perhaps the only tangible outcome) of St. Louis 2004 ("Tale of Two Playgrounds" 2004) is the continuing development of a regional greenway network that has become a national model (Britt 2004).

## Phase 1: The 2004 Initiative

In 1996 the Danforth Foundation provided funding to establish St. Louis 2004. St. Louis 2004's mission was to engage the St. Louis community in celebrating milestone historical events and to position the metropolitan area to more successfully compete in a global marketplace. The funding enabled the hiring of a savvy professional staff. Initially led by JoAnne LaSala, a former budget director for the City of St. Louis, LaSala was succeeded in late 1999 by Peter Sortino, a key staff member in two City of St. Louis administrations (*St. Louis Business Journal* 1999). From St. Louis 2004's inception its mission was to stimulate change during the time period 1996 to 2004 and then to terminate. It was described as "a revival, not an organization" (*St. Louis Business Journal* 2001).

In 1996 and 1997, St. Louis 2004 conducted a visioning process that engaged a broad base of people in looking to the future of the region. A public opinion poll identified topics of concern and opportunities for transformation. The poll results were scrutinized by 6 action teams, 29 committees, and more than 1,200 volunteers. In follow-up a series of fifty community forums drew 1,500 participants. The forums resulted in thirteen initiatives that surfaced as regional priorities, such as downtown and neighborhood revitalization, access to health care, and after-school programs (Trust for Public Land 2001).

One of the clear results of the polling and priority setting was an interest in green space and clean water. The 2004 Parks and Open Space Task Force sustained the development of this initiative. In addition to the citizen representatives who participated in the committees and community forums, community leaders and local park professionals were included on the Parks and Open Space Task Force. The work of the Task Force was enhanced by specialty consulting services. The Conservation Fund, the Trust for Public Land, and Glazer and Associates assisted in developing strategies that applied the responses solicited from the community in the public opinion polls and forums (American Trails 1997).

The Task Force identified creating a bi-state system of linear parks and trails revolving around area rivers as a priority to improve the quality of life in the St. Louis region. Such a park system would require funding, for which support had been indicated in the polling. A regional system would require authorizing legislation to set up a special district.

## Phase 2: The Legislative Initiative

St. Louis had gotten this far nearly a century before. However, this time the scale was larger. Instead of the City and the County, it was to be a bi-state effort. This time the initiative was not led by civic volunteers. In January 1999, St. Louis 2004 established a special-purpose nonprofit organization, Greenway Parks and Trails 2004, for the short-term purpose of leading the legislative initiative. Robert J. Hall, who had just retired as director of the St. Louis County parks department, was named executive director. Hall, a nationally recognized parks executive, assumed responsibility for melding citizen input and quality planning into a passable ballot initiative (*St. Louis Business Journal* 2000).

Greenway Parks and Trails 2004 had two tasks—to shape the vision of the Parks and Open Space Task Force, and to develop a coalition of interests strong enough to support legislative approval for a metropolitan taxing jurisdiction. There needed to be two levels of engagement in the second task.

With more than sixty local jurisdictions already supporting park facilities, Greenway Parks and Trails 2004 needed a compelling strategy for supporting a new open-space initiative. Through extensive meetings and negotiations with parks staff and elected officials, a revenue-sharing proposal developed. Part of the funds raised by the regional district would go to the district, and part would go to local agencies, both county and municipal. Rather than the traditional call for consolidating or eliminating existing multiple authorities, Gateway Parks and Trails 2004 garnered the support for its regional vision from county and municipal officials.

In addition to the revenue-sharing strategy, Gateway Parks and Trails 2004 contracted the HOK Planning Group to prepare a master plan to clarify the concept of a regional greenway network. The working plan at this phase was two hundred miles of trails radiating out from a circular centralized trail, looking rather like a hub with spokes connecting to an outer wheel (HOK Planning Group 2004).

Gateway Parks and Trails 2004 became an advocate with both citizens and legislators to gain acceptance of the revenue-sharing plan and the master plan. In May 1999, the Illinois and Missouri general assemblies passed legislation allowing voters to approve park and recreation districts and a one-tenth of one-cent sales tax to fund the districts. On July 13, 1999, Missouri and Illinois governors signed legislation authorizing the nation's first local, bi-state park and recreation districts.[4]

The legislation incorporated the revenue-sharing plan. Under the plan, the metropolitan district would receive 50 percent of the tax proceeds. Each county would receive 50 percent of the revenues collected within its jurisdiction. Municipal projects would be funded through an application process that would garner 40 percent of each county's share of the tax revenue.

Acknowledging the dynamics of population movement in the St. Louis region, the legislation states that the composition of the district governing

---

[4] Missouri Revised Statutes (RSMo) 67.1700–67.1769; problems of multi-county jurisdiction addressed in revisions to state law. See Section 67.750.
http://www.moga.mo.gov/statutesearch/.

body could be altered in 2012 and every ten years thereafter. This would allow time for publication of the 2010 census and schedule governing structure review to coincide with future census releases.

## Phase 3: The Ballot Initiative

Having negotiated support from the park professionals and won approval of the legislatures, Greenway Parks and Trails 2004 next needed approval from a majority of voters to establish the district and provide the revenue. Three strategies in particular were important to the outcome of the election.

First, this phase drew extensively on work done in the prior phases. For example, the ballot wording and the title of the proposition carefully chose concepts and terms that had received strong positive responses in the prior citizen input. Proposition C: The Clean Water, Safe Parks and Community Trails Initiative was not just a name, it articulated a message. The design work presented a clear picture of the impact of the two hundred miles of greenway trails.

Second, the proposed district would not be the only financial beneficiary of the sales tax. As locally negotiated, and then authorized in the legislation, half of the tax proceeds would go to existing park departments—giving them a stake in the outcome of the election.

And third, the proposition was put on the November 2000 ballot. Because the 2000 election was a presidential election, it was chosen because it would draw the highest turnout with the best chance to reflect general community sentiment.

With support from St. Louis 2004, Greenway Parks and Trails 2004 was successful in raising $1.5 million to support the campaign effort. While a presidential election assured a large community turnout, it also assured a lot of competition for voters' attention. A large amount of the resources was reserved for intense publicity in the last two weeks before the election. Publicity for Proposition C included direct mail and television, radio, and print advertisements (*St. Louis Business Journal*, 2000).

On November 7, 2000, Proposition C, the Clean Water, Safe Parks and Community Trails Initiative, was on the ballot in seven counties, three in Missouri and four in Illinois. It passed overwhelmingly in all three Missouri counties and in two of the four Illinois counties, creating the Metropolitan Park and Recreation District in Missouri and the Metro-East Park and Recreation District in Illinois.[5]

---

[5] The proposition was approved in Missouri by 76.5 percent of the voters in the City of St. Louis, 69.6 percent of St. Louis County voters, and 56.7 percent in St. Charles County. In Illinois 61.5 percent of St. Clair County voters approved it, as did 51.2 percent of Monroe County voters. It did not get a simple majority in Clinton and Madison counties.

With the successful passage of Proposition C, the work of Greenway Parks and Trails 2004 was complete, and the work of implementing the plans transitioned to the new districts.

## Phase 4: The Planning Initiative

The Missouri district progressed rapidly after voter approval.[6] The District began receiving sales tax revenue in April 2001. A policy board of the Metropolitan Park and Recreation District (MPRD) had met in February 2001 to initiate the process of incorporating the district. As delineated in the enabling legislation, the chief elected official of the City of St. Louis, St. Louis County, and St. Charles County appointed members to the MPRD board of directors. There are ten members on the MPRD board: two from St. Charles County, three from the City of St. Louis, and five from St. Louis County.

The board appointed David Fisher executive director in November 2001. Fisher's previous experience included seventeen years as superintendent of the Minneapolis Park and Recreation Board. Fisher was responsible for a number of riverfront and neighborhood park initiatives there. He received the National Gold Medal Award for Excellence in Park and Recreation Management in 1989 from the National Park and Recreation Association.

With its funding and professional staff in place, the MPRD initiated a planning process. As was the case with the process that resulted in its formation, citizen input and professional consultation were core elements of the early actions of the district (Antoine 2004). In late 2002, the MPRD established a thirty-seven-member Citizens' Advisory Committee (CAC). Working with the staff and professional consultants (Figure 2), the CAC conducted a two-step process of information gathering. The communications team prepared and facilitated CAC meetings and public hearings. The planning team conducted research, did design work, and developed the collaborative plan. Internally, it identified both assets and liabilities. To broaden the base of input, the CAC held approximately thirty focus group meetings attended by over 250 residents from the three counties. A fifty-member Technical Advisory Committee (TAC) supported the CAC over the course of its ten-month process, completed in September 2003 (Antoine 2002).

---

[6] The balance of this chapter concentrates on the Metropolitan Park and Recreation District established in Missouri. While conceived as a regional initiative, the funding reality is the Missouri district generates approximately $10 million a year from its 50 percent share of the sales tax and the Illinois district $1.5 million. With fewer resources there has been substantially less planning and activity in the Illinois district.

As Searns noted, contemporary greenways are multi-objective. The MPRD identified three objectives for its projects: economic development, environmental stewardship, and social capital. Termed "driving principals" in the planning process, the MPRD planned significant impact beyond the recreational potential of the greenway system:

**Figure 2. Metropolitan Park and Recreation District**

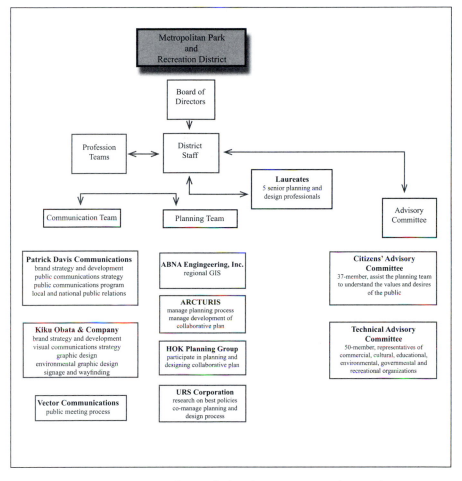

*Economic Development*—planned developments, parks, and open space are known to enhance surrounding urban development (Crompton 2001; Lutzenhiser and Netusil 2001). A linear park or greenway connects a substantial number of private properties to planned and maintained open space. The goals of the MPRD are not only to increase property values, but also to stimulate redevelopment in existing neighborhoods by establishing a regional network of greenways.

*Environmental Stewardship*—the language in Proposition C stated the regional park district would improve air and water quality. MPRD's environmental goals for the greenway network are to create access to rivers and their immediate landscape and through the improved access to enhance awareness of environmental issues. In addition, the greenways would protect aquatic and wildlife habitats.

*Social Capital*—the greenway system was conceived to enhance both property worth and personal and community worth, not only in financial terms but also in terms of education, health, and stronger community bonds. The greenway trails provide expansive facilities for educating children and adults about the flora and fauna of the riverine systems, facilities for physical activity, and, opportunities for cultural diversity. One issue that frequently surfaced within the CAC and in its outreach activities was the ability of the St. Louis region to attract and retain younger citizens. Metropolitan areas successful in expanding their population base with age groups in the twenties and thirties often are noted for their social and recreational quality of life. The development of a major regional greenway system is, among other things, intended to give St. Louis a competitive edge.

# River Ring: Plan Implementation

Perhaps the two most important outcomes of the planning process were a new identity and a signature project for the MPRD. The MPRD began to do business in mid-2003 as Great Rivers Greenway (GRG).[7] This name was approved by the MPRD in an effort to operate under a moniker that would be descriptive of its mission as well as reinforce an image as a participatory citizens' organization, not a formal government body.

GRG's signature project is the River Ring, an ambitious undertaking. Its development will span decades. As shown in Map 3, the River Ring encompasses an area of approximately 1,200 square miles. It scope is grand not only in scale but also in purpose. "The development of the River Ring will create a new sense of place and a source of pride" (Antoine 2002).

---

[7] Not to be confused with Great River Greenway, a St. Paul, Minnesota, reforestation program.

Map 3. The River Ring

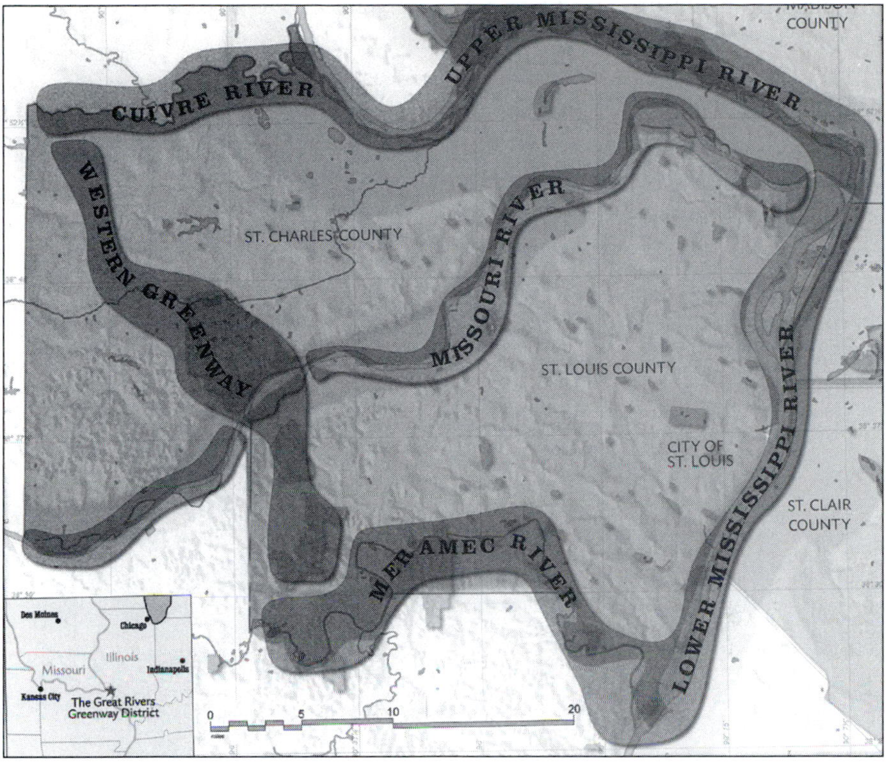

Source: Great Rivers Greenway.

The River Ring seeks to add a new dimension to Hamilton's list of open space benefits—creating an image that is known and respected within St. Louis as well as nationally and internationally. It took eighty years after the Outer Park Plan and twenty years after the Gateway Discovery Trail for another initiative to realize the vision of both these efforts, and then some. There are structural and functional aspects that determine both the short- and long-term success of realizing this vision.

## Structure
The River Ring is an outside boundary for a six-hundred-mile network of forty-five greenways.[8] It will be developed in three layers: regional, local, and neighborhood.

---

[8] The River Ring was initially planned to be implemented by watershed districts, but that plan was terminated by a change in Missouri law. See Section 67.1706 of RSMo.

There are thirteen regional greenways that are the major corridors on the perimeter of and within the River Ring. Regional greenways are the longest continuous components of the network along the banks of the Mississippi, Missouri, Meramec, and Cuivre rivers.

The thirty-two local greenways are primarily on river tributaries, in many cases connecting to one another to establish the network of trails throughout the region or connecting to schools and natural, cultural, historic, and community resources. The local greenways will be of particular significance in returning the community to the riverian environment. They will graphically demonstrate the connection to the major waterways yet provide immediate access in neighborhoods throughout the region.

Neighborhood greenways frequently are shortcuts that connect smaller sections of regional greenways or connect one or more local greenways to a regional greenway. In many places they will connect existing neighborhood parks or trails to the newly developed greenways. There are potentially hundreds of neighborhood greenway projects.

The plan includes extensive analysis and description of confluences. Confluences are the intersections of the various levels of greenways and will provide the primary access points as well as locations for parking, rental of bicycles and electric-powered vehicles for the elderly and disabled, and large information kiosks.

## Function

The impetus for branding the regional park district to engage citizen awareness and interest was critical because there will be separate planning processes for each of these greenways. While there will be continuous need for professional consultation services in environmental analysis and facilities planning, the development of the greenways will be incremental, taking each year's allocation of funds and setting priorities for individual projects. GRG is restricting the use of its funds primarily to capital development activity, so for each project it must negotiate with a local authority for maintenance of the greenways and their facilities.

GRG is integrating its work with that of local authorities through SEED (social, environmental, and economic development) projects. As of July 2005, GRG initiated twenty SEED projects in ten different greenways. While the majority are projects on the major rivers, there is significant activity on tributary creeks and streams throughout the GRG service area.

The Meramec River and River Des Peres greenways are early examples of River Ring SEED projects that implement the guiding principles established in the GRG planning process. The Meramec River Greenway has been a vision of a number of community interests for more than thirty years.[9] While various resources, developed plans, and scattered parcels of land along the riverian corridor were acquired, there was no stable funding for facility development (St. Louis County, 2003). GRG has provided the financing for a "backbone" trail that is intended to become a significant tourist destination in the primarily rural areas traversed by the Meramec River. To enhance the economic development potential of recreational tourism in the Meramec Greenway, GRG funded marketing media including a print brochure and a Web site. This greenway project also will fulfill the purpose of environmental stewardship through the removal of residential and commercial structures in the Meramec River floodplain, assuring that storm water runoff into the river is relatively clean. GRG has partnered with St. Louis County, the Corps of Engineers, and the Meramec River Recreation Association in planning and developing the Meramec River Greenway project.

The River Des Peres Greenway has significant potential for urban economic development impact. From Forest Park to its mouth at the Mississippi River, the banks of the River Des Peres adjoin intensely built-up commercial, industrial, and residential property. As was the case with so many initiatives prior to GRG, a conceptual plan was funded and a number of agencies agreed on a goal for a riverian open space. For the River Des Peres Greenway this included the City of St. Louis, St. Louis County, the Army Corps of Engineers, and the Metropolitan St. Louis Sewer District reaching consensus on the long-term goal of increasing property values and economic development opportunities in the Lemay area of south St. Louis County and in south St. Louis City. GRG funded a pilot project developing pedestrian bridges, signalized lighting for crossing all streets, lighting along the greenway, benches, landscaping, and a new trailhead. The impact of these improvements (estimated at over $5 million) will provide an early indication of the potential for the River Ring to affect surrounding property values on or near its greenways.

GRG is perhaps unique among the many greenway development agencies in the United States in its commitment to developing social capital. An example is the Visitor and Education Center in Forest Park. Forest Park Forever, a nonprofit organization responsible for raising the

---

[9] The concept of a greenway for the Meramec River developed in the mid-1970s after cancellation of a proposed Army Corps of Engineers dam.

funds to renovate Forest Park, the largest single open space in the City of St. Louis, requested funds from GRG convert a 1904-era pavilion to a resource center where residents could gather together and visitors and users could obtain information on the numerous recreational, cultural, and education opportunities found throughout the park. Offices for Forest Park Forever, OASIS St. Louis, and the Missouri Department of Conservation are located in the center, with volunteers from the St. Louis Convention and Visitors Commission working the visitor information area. Located along the popular trails and adjacent to the handball and racquetball courts, the center serves as the trailhead for the park and provides restrooms, lockers, and shower facilities for recreational users.

# Beyond Open Space

The Gateway Arch has the advantage of being not only a national monument but also a readily reproducible logo and tagline that has innumerable applications in the St. Louis region. While the River Ring may not find the same utility in marketing symbolism, it will create a physical connection among St. Louis neighborhoods that has never existed and an image of accomplishment and vitality that will have many benefits. In addition to its direct impact, there can be lessons learned from the process that brought it from an idea to a reality.

Just as the river gives St. Louis a sense of something larger than itself, the hope is for the River Ring to provide a better region in other aspects than just open space. As Robert Hall said, "the metropolitan park districts for Missouri and Illinois will give the St. Louis community the opportunity to truly come together on a regional issue, which could set the tone for similar cooperation in the future" (*St. Louis Business Journal*, 2000).

**Acknowledgments**
The author thanks the staff of Great Rivers Greenway for preparing information on the SEED projects described in this chapter; also, thanks to Rebecca Pastor for review and comments on (several) drafts.

# References

American Trails. "St. Louis 2004 Regional Park and Greenway System," October 1997. http://americantrails.org/resources/greenways/GrnwyStLouis2004.html (accessed June 29, 2005).

Anderson, Tom. "Businesses Blazing Path to Pass Tax for Trail District." *St. Louis Business Journal*, September 15, 2000. http://www.bizjournals.com/stlouis/stories/2000/09/18/story4.html.

Antoine, Todd. *Collaborating with Citizens and Communities: Creating an Interlinked, Regional System of Greenways, Parks and Trails*. St. Louis: Great Rivers Greenway District, 2002.

———. "Planning an Interconnected System of Greenways, Parks and Trails for the St. Louis Region." *American Planning Association of Missouri Newsletter*, Winter 2004, pp. 8–15.

Britt, Sue. "Lord of the (River) Rings." *St. Louis Commerce Magazine*, November 1, 2004. http://www.stlcommercemagazine.com/archives/november2004/rings.html.

Civic League of St. Louis. *Inner and Outer Parks and Boulevards: A Complete System Connecting Existing Parks and Forest Reservations in the County*. St. Louis: Author, 1907.

Corbett, Katharine T. "Draining the Metropolis." In *Common Fields*, edited by Andrew Hurley. St. Louis: Missouri Historical Society Press, 1997.

Crompton, John L. "The Impact of Parks on Property Values: A Review of the Empirical Evidence." *Journal of Leisure Research* 33 (2001): 1–31.

Fabos, Julius Gy. "Introduction and Overview: The Greenway Movement, Uses, and Potentials of Greenways." In *Greenways: The Beginning of an International Movement*, edited by Julius Gy. Fabos and Jack Ahern. Amsterdam: Elsevier, 1996.

Garvin, Alexander, and Gayle Berens. *Urban Parks and Open Space*. Washington, DC: Urban Land Institute, 1997.

Greater Saint Louis Committee. *The Public Reservation (or Outer Park) Plan for St. Louis City and County*. St. Louis: Author, 1914.

Hamilton, Leonard W., ed. *The Benefits of Open Space*. Madison, NJ: Great Swamp Watershed Association, 1997. http://www.greatswamp.org/publications/benefits.htm.

HOK Planning Group. *Portfolio: Gateway Parks and Trails 2004*. http://www.hokplanninggroup.com/projects/portfolio/index2.htm.

Kent, Fred, and Kathy Madden. "Creating Great Urban Parks." Project for Public Spaces, 1998. http://www.pps.org/topics/design/CreatingUrbanParks.

Lindsey, Greg. "Sustainability and Urban Greenways." *APA Journal* (Spring 2003).

Little, Charles E. *Greenways for America*. Baltimore: Johns Hopkins University Press, 1995.

Lutzenhiser, Margot, and Noelwah R. Netusil. "The Effect of Open Spaces on a Home's Sale Price." *Contemporary Economic Policy* 19, no. 3 (2001): 291–298.

Metropolitan Research and Services Center of Washington. "Metropolitan Parks Districts," 2004. http://www.mrsc.org/subjects/parks/SPD-MPD.aspx.

Missouri Department of Conservation. *Impacts of Development on Waterways*. Jefferson City, MO: Author, 2004.

Norris, F. Terry. "Where Did the Villages Go?" In *Common Fields*, edited by Andrew Hurley. St. Louis: Missouri Historical Society Press, 1997.

Olshansky, Robert. "Planning for Public Parks." *APA Journal* 69, no. 3 (Spring 2003): 318.

Primm, James Neal. *Lion of the Valley*. 3rd ed. St. Louis: Missouri Historical Society Press, 1998.

Schwarz, Loring LaB., ed. *Greenways*. Washington, DC: Island Press, 1993.

Searns, R. M. "The Evolution of Greenways as an Adaptive Urban Landscape Form." *Landscape and Urban Planning* 33 (1995): 65–80.

Shriver, Katherine. "On the Trail of Funding Alternatives." *Parks and Recreation* 33, no. 7 (1998).

*St. Louis Business Journal*. "LaSala Steps Down as President, Takes on Consulting Role at St. Louis 2004." *St. Louis Business Journal*, December 24, 1999. http://www.bizjournals.com/stlouis/stories/1999/12/27/story6.html.

———. "100 Leaders for the New Millennium." *St. Louis Business Journal*, January 28, 2000. http://www.bizjournals.com/stlouis/stories/2000/01/31/focus32.html.

———. "St. Louis 2004 Status at the Midway Point." *St. Louis Business Journal*, February 9, 2001.

St. Louis County. "St. Louis County Meramec River Greenway Concept Plan, September 2003." St. Louis: Author, 2003.

"Tale of Two Playgrounds Shows Civic Group's Impact." *St. Louis Post-Dispatch*, May 23, 2004, special section, p. 3.

Trust for Public Land. "Case Studies—St. Louis Metro Region—The Clean Water, Safe Parks, and Community Trails Initiative," 2005. http://www.tpl.org/tier3_cdl.cfm?content_item_id=4528&folder_id=1365.

United States Army Corps of Engineers, St. Louis District. *St. Louis Metropolitan Area, Missouri and Illinois Study*. St. Louis: Author, 1977.

# Appendix

## Selected Economic and Social Indicators for the 50 Largest Metropolitan Areas, 1990–2000

| | Percent Black | | Percent Hispanic | | Percent Immigrants | |
|---|---|---|---|---|---|---|
| | 1990 | 2000 | 1990 | 2000 | 1990 | 2000 |
| Atlanta | 25.98 | 28.92 | 2.02 | 6.54 | 1.55 | 4.22 |
| Austin | 9.24 | 7.96 | 20.46 | 26.23 | 2.59 | 4.44 |
| Boston | 5.73 | 5.14 | 4.63 | 6.16 | 2.78 | 3.30 |
| Buffalo | 10.25 | 11.71 | 2.05 | 2.90 | 0.75 | 1.06 |
| Charlotte | 19.93 | 20.54 | 0.92 | 5.14 | 0.80 | 2.27 |
| Chicago | 19.19 | 18.65 | 11.08 | 16.36 | 2.27 | 2.94 |
| Cincinnati | 11.67 | 11.67 | 0.54 | 1.14 | 0.57 | 3.73 |
| Cleveland | 16.01 | 16.75 | 1.92 | 2.74 | 0.69 | 1.17 |
| Columbus | 11.95 | 13.38 | 0.82 | 1.83 | 1.06 | 1.19 |
| Dallas | 14.27 | 13.79 | 13.36 | 21.46 | 2.12 | 2.16 |
| Denver | 5.29 | 4.64 | 12.24 | 18.46 | 1.60 | 4.78 |
| Detroit | 20.90 | 21.06 | 1.95 | 2.86 | 1.02 | 3.90 |
| Grand Rapids | 6.00 | 7.29 | 3.29 | 6.33 | 0.77 | 2.11 |
| Greensboro | 19.35 | 20.19 | 0.75 | 4.97 | 0.64 | 2.62 |
| Hartford | 8.74 | 9.45 | 6.96 | 9.60 | 1.53 | 2.29 |
| Houston | 17.93 | 16.91 | 20.81 | 28.88 | 2.78 | 4.95 |
| Indianapolis | 13.79 | 13.93 | 0.89 | 2.67 | 0.68 | 1.57 |
| Jacksonville | 19.99 | 21.67 | 2.48 | 3.83 | 1.33 | 2.08 |
| Kansas City | 12.80 | 12.75 | 2.89 | 5.23 | 0.94 | 1.90 |
| Las Vegas | 9.54 | 8.07 | 11.18 | 20.60 | 2.93 | 4.27 |
| Los Angeles | 8.46 | 7.60 | 32.89 | 40.30 | 6.69 | 4.61 |
| Louisville | 13.10 | 13.92 | 0.61 | 1.61 | 0.49 | 1.38 |
| Memphis | 40.64 | 43.37 | 0.81 | 2.42 | 0.60 | 1.68 |
| Miami | 18.53 | 20.39 | 33.26 | 40.33 | 6.45 | 7.88 |
| Milwaukee | 13.33 | 15.08 | 3.75 | 6.48 | 0.74 | 1.60 |
| Minneapolis | 3.64 | 5.32 | 1.52 | 3.34 | 1.22 | 2.37 |
| Nashville | 15.47 | 15.58 | 0.78 | 3.26 | 0.81 | 2.14 |
| New Orleans | 34.75 | 37.55 | 4.30 | 4.38 | 0.86 | 1.19 |
| New York | 18.19 | 17.16 | 15.36 | 18.17 | 4.11 | 4.73 |
| Norfolk | 28.51 | 30.92 | 2.32 | 3.12 | 2.38 | 2.25 |
| Oklahoma City | 10.54 | 10.56 | 3.56 | 6.74 | 1.27 | 2.26 |
| Orlando | 12.43 | 13.86 | 8.99 | 16.52 | 1.87 | 3.55 |
| Philadelphia | 18.65 | 19.57 | 3.83 | 5.63 | 1.21 | 1.96 |
| Phoenix | 3.50 | 3.68 | 16.28 | 25.12 | 2.20 | 4.47 |
| Pittsburgh | 7.97 | 8.08 | 0.57 | 0.72 | 0.49 | 0.96 |
| Portland | 2.82 | 2.39 | 3.38 | 8.68 | 1.74 | 3.46 |
| Providence | 3.25 | 3.96 | 4.16 | 7.90 | 1.89 | 2.02 |
| Raleigh | 24.94 | 22.72 | 1.23 | 6.11 | 1.75 | 4.27 |
| Richmond | 29.15 | 30.15 | 1.08 | 2.34 | 1.02 | 1.83 |
| Rochester | 9.36 | 10.26 | 3.12 | 4.33 | 0.95 | 1.47 |
| Sacramento | 6.88 | 7.13 | 11.64 | 15.48 | 2.61 | 3.31 |
| Salt Lake City | 0.98 | 1.11 | 5.78 | 10.84 | 1.50 | 3.51 |
| San Antonio | 6.82 | 6.63 | 47.64 | 51.25 | 2.35 | 2.64 |
| San Diego | 6.38 | 5.74 | 20.45 | 26.69 | 4.87 | 4.13 |
| San Francisco | 8.60 | 7.30 | 15.52 | 19.66 | 4.98 | 5.65 |
| Seattle | 4.82 | 4.67 | 2.95 | 5.18 | 2.62 | 3.66 |
| St. Louis | 17.31 | 18.31 | 1.06 | 1.52 | 0.83 | 1.44 |
| Tampa | 8.97 | 10.20 | 6.73 | 10.38 | 1.49 | 2.62 |
| Washington | 26.56 | 26.19 | 5.73 | 6.37 | 5.10 | 4.18 |
| West Palm Beach | 12.47 | 13.80 | 7.71 | 12.44 | 2.42 | 4.16 |

Source: U.S. Bureau of the Census.

| | Population | | Median Household Income | |
|---|---|---|---|---|
| | 1990 | 2000 | 1990 | 2000 |
| Atlanta | 2,833,511 | 4,112,198 | 36,051 | 51,948 |
| Austin | 781,572 | 1,249,763 | 28,474 | 48,950 |
| Boston | 4,171,643 | 5,819,100 | 40,666 | 52,792 |
| Buffalo | 1,189,288 | 1,170,111 | 28,084 | 38,488 |
| Charlotte | 1,162,093 | 1,499,293 | 31,125 | 46,732 |
| Chicago | 8,065,633 | 9,157,540 | 35,918 | 46,119 |
| Cincinnati | 1,744,124 | 1,979,202 | 30,977 | 51,046 |
| Cleveland | 2,759,823 | 2,945,831 | 30,332 | 44,914 |
| Columbus | 1,377,419 | 1,540,157 | 30,668 | 42,215 |
| Dallas | 3,885,415 | 5,221,801 | 32,825 | 44,782 |
| Denver | 1,848,319 | 2,581,506 | 33,126 | 47,418 |
| Detroit | 4,665,236 | 5,456,428 | 34,729 | 51,088 |
| Grand Rapids | 688,399 | 1,088,514 | 33,515 | 49,160 |
| Greensboro | 942,091 | 1,251,509 | 29,254 | 40,913 |
| Hartford | 1,085,837 | 1,183,110 | 41,440 | 52,188 |
| Houston | 3,711,043 | 4,669,571 | 31,488 | 44,761 |
| Indianapolis | 1,249,822 | 1,607,486 | 31,655 | 45,548 |
| Jacksonville | 906,727 | 1,100,491 | 29,514 | 42,439 |
| Kansas City | 1,566,280 | 1,776,062 | 31,613 | 46,193 |
| Las Vegas | 741,459 | 1,563,282 | 30,746 | 42,468 |
| Los Angeles | 14,531,529 | 16,373,645 | 36,711 | 45,903 |
| Louisville | 952,662 | 1,025,598 | 27,599 | 40,821 |
| Memphis | 981,747 | 1,135,614 | 26,994 | 40,201 |
| Miami | 3,192,582 | 3,876,380 | 28,503 | 38,632 |
| Milwaukee | 1,607,183 | 1,689,572 | 32,359 | 46,132 |
| Minneapolis | 2,464,124 | 2,968,806 | 36,565 | 54,304 |
| Nashville | 985,026 | 1,231,311 | 30,223 | 44,223 |
| New Orleans | 1,238,816 | 1,337,726 | 24,442 | 35,317 |
| New York | 18,087,251 | 21,199,865 | 38,445 | 50,795 |
| Norfolk | 1,396,107 | 1,569,541 | 30,841 | 42,448 |
| Oklahoma City | 958,839 | 1,083,346 | 26,883 | 36,797 |
| Orlando | 1,072,748 | 1,644,561 | 31,230 | 41,871 |
| Philadelphia | 5,899,345 | 6,188,463 | 35,797 | 47,528 |
| Phoenix | 2,122,101 | 3,251,876 | 30,797 | 44,752 |
| Pittsburgh | 2,242,798 | 2,358,695 | 26,501 | 37,467 |
| Portland | 1,477,895 | 2,265,223 | 31,071 | 46,090 |
| Providence | 1,141,510 | 1,188,613 | 31,858 | 41,748 |
| Raleigh | 735,480 | 1,187,941 | 33,290 | 48,845 |
| Richmond | 865,640 | 996,512 | 33,489 | 46,800 |
| Rochester | 1,002,410 | 1,098,201 | 34,234 | 43,955 |
| Sacramento | 1,481,102 | 1,796,857 | 32,734 | 46,106 |
| Salt Lake City | 1,072,227 | 1,333,914 | 30,882 | 48,594 |
| San Antonio | 1,302,099 | 1,592,383 | 26,092 | 39,140 |
| San Diego | 2,498,016 | 2,813,833 | 35,022 | 47,067 |
| San Francisco | 6,253,311 | 7,039,362 | 41,459 | 62,024 |
| Seattle | 2,559,164 | 3,554,760 | 35,047 | 50,733 |
| St. Louis | 2,444,099 | 2,603,607 | 31,774 | 44,437 |
| Tampa | 2,067,959 | 2,395,997 | 26,036 | 37,406 |
| Washington | 3,923,574 | 7,608,070 | 46,884 | 57,291 |
| West Palm Beach | 863,518 | 1,131,184 | 32,524 | 45,062 |

| Percent College | | Percent Poor | | Percent Unemployed | |
|---|---|---|---|---|---|
| 1990 | 2000 | 1990 | 2000 | 1990 | 2000 |
| 26.78 | 32.05 | 10.04 | 9.40 | 5.13 | 5.01 |
| 32.24 | 36.69 | 15.30 | 11.07 | 5.82 | 4.03 |
| 30.66 | 34.39 | 8.11 | 8.56 | 6.44 | 4.25 |
| 18.82 | 23.21 | 11.96 | 11.88 | 6.99 | 7.04 |
| 19.59 | 26.47 | 9.60 | 8.61 | 4.02 | 3.93 |
| 23.49 | 28.89 | 11.32 | 9.34 | 6.80 | 5.22 |
| 20.22 | 25.02 | 11.31 | 10.50 | 5.17 | 6.26 |
| 19.05 | 23.54 | 11.84 | 9.52 | 6.67 | 4.25 |
| 23.00 | 29.05 | 11.82 | 10.58 | 5.15 | 5.18 |
| 25.84 | 28.37 | 11.70 | 10.08 | 5.75 | 4.05 |
| 30.47 | 35.46 | 9.88 | 10.83 | 5.26 | 4.77 |
| 19.09 | 23.70 | 12.84 | 8.55 | 8.48 | 4.10 |
| 20.18 | 22.91 | 8.29 | 10.64 | 4.96 | 5.77 |
| 19.23 | 22.88 | 9.98 | 10.41 | 4.26 | 4.72 |
| 25.98 | 29.79 | 7.08 | 8.38 | 4.90 | 5.73 |
| 24.19 | 26.51 | 14.88 | 13.67 | 6.70 | 6.21 |
| 21.10 | 25.83 | 9.60 | 8.57 | 4.75 | 4.39 |
| 18.58 | 22.87 | 11.85 | 10.67 | 5.43 | 4.72 |
| 23.37 | 28.50 | 9.81 | 8.47 | 5.47 | 4.27 |
| 13.81 | 16.39 | 10.53 | 11.07 | 6.70 | 6.60 |
| 21.98 | 24.39 | 13.09 | 15.62 | 6.78 | 7.42 |
| 17.34 | 22.17 | 12.69 | 10.90 | 5.97 | 4.64 |
| 18.96 | 22.69 | 18.31 | 15.34 | 7.24 | 6.39 |
| 18.77 | 22.91 | 14.88 | 15.25 | 6.76 | 7.24 |
| 20.77 | 26.20 | 11.43 | 10.36 | 5.48 | 5.32 |
| 27.13 | 33.26 | 8.07 | 6.71 | 4.60 | 3.50 |
| 21.39 | 26.85 | 11.33 | 10.10 | 4.84 | 4.48 |
| 19.75 | 22.56 | 21.21 | 18.38 | 9.22 | 6.80 |
| 25.77 | 30.50 | 11.65 | 12.90 | 6.74 | 6.67 |
| 20.12 | 23.80 | 11.46 | 10.63 | 6.04 | 5.67 |
| 21.62 | 24.45 | 13.92 | 13.54 | 6.55 | 4.83 |
| 21.59 | 24.80 | 9.96 | 10.68 | 4.75 | 4.59 |
| 22.79 | 26.88 | 10.07 | 10.88 | 5.60 | 6.25 |
| 22.13 | 25.08 | 12.33 | 12.01 | 6.05 | 4.88 |
| 18.89 | 23.84 | 12.27 | 10.81 | 7.04 | 5.81 |
| 23.59 | 27.65 | 9.88 | 10.02 | 5.11 | 5.89 |
| 19.60 | 23.62 | 9.52 | 11.78 | 6.86 | 5.51 |
| 34.76 | 38.91 | 10.23 | 10.25 | 3.72 | 4.10 |
| 23.81 | 29.21 | 9.76 | 9.27 | 4.18 | 4.16 |
| 23.42 | 27.10 | 9.75 | 10.33 | 5.15 | 5.74 |
| 23.35 | 26.55 | 11.89 | 12.75 | 6.09 | 6.22 |
| 22.89 | 26.53 | 9.42 | 7.66 | 4.90 | 4.74 |
| 19.44 | 22.45 | 19.49 | 15.08 | 8.33 | 5.71 |
| 25.29 | 29.52 | 11.34 | 12.43 | 6.11 | 5.93 |
| 30.87 | 37.25 | 8.62 | 8.72 | 5.19 | 4.54 |
| 27.15 | 31.98 | 8.48 | 8.54 | 4.60 | 5.11 |
| 20.73 | 25.33 | 10.75 | 9.95 | 6.38 | 5.51 |
| 17.29 | 21.69 | 11.39 | 11.15 | 5.22 | 4.97 |
| 38.46 | 37.10 | 6.45 | 8.26 | 3.70 | 4.52 |
| 22.13 | 27.71 | 9.30 | 9.92 | 5.15 | 4.96 |

# Index